The Secret Lives of
Sgt. John Wilson

A True Story of Love & Murder

Lois Simmie

GREYSTONE BOOKS
Douglas & McIntyre
Vancouver / Toronto

95 96 97 98 99   5 4 3 2

Greystone Books
A division of Douglas & McIntyre Ltd.
1615 Venables Street
Vancouver, British Columbia
V5L 2H1

Canadian Cataloguing in Publication Data

Simmie, Lois, 1932 –
  The secret lives of Sgt. John Wilson

  ISBN 1-55054-442-X
  1. Wilson, John, d. 1920.   2. Murderers – Saskatchewan –
Biography.   3. Uxoricide – Saskatchewan.   I. Title.
HV6542.S55 1995   364.1'523'092   C95-910350-3

Editing by Jennifer Glossop
Cover and text design by DesignGeist
Typeset by Val Speidel
Printed and bound in Canada by Friesens
Printed on acid-free paper ∞

The author gratefully acknowledges the support of the Canada Council.

The publisher gratefully acknowledges the assistance of the Canada Council and of the British Columbia Ministry of Tourism, Small Business and Culture through its publishing programs.

The John Wilson story is a true one. Scenes in this book are based closely on real events and situations, and on my understanding of the characters and happenings as revealed in letters, statements, police reports and eyewitness accounts.

Although great care was taken not to attribute to the characters suggestive thoughts or dialogue unless substantiated by evidence, in many cases thoughts and speech are based on what I believe would be natural in the situation. All the letters, reports and other documents are genuine, though some have been shortened, and spelling and punctuation have been corrected for ease of reading.

This story has fascinated me for a long time, and I finally was compelled to write it.

Lois Simmie

To the memory of Polly Wilson, 1886–1918

To the memory of my father, Ed Binns, 1897–1960

I am a maid that sleeps in love and cannot tell my pain,
For once I had a sweetheart and Johnny was his name.
And if I cannot find him, I'll wander night and day,
And it's for the sake of Johnny I'll cross the stormy seas.

From "I Am a Maid That Sleeps in Love,"
an old ballad, author unknown

We were as God made us, and oftentimes even worse.

Unknown mounted policeman, quoted in *The
Mounties: The History of the RCMP* by Jim Lotz

ᗣ ACKNOWLEDGEMENTS ᗧ

There are many people to thank for assistance with this book. Lynn Hudson gave generously of his knowledge and supplied the cover photographs and others. His historical booklet *Murder in Uniform*, co-authored by Christina Stewart, started me on this odyssey. Thanks to Glenn Wright, historian at the Ottawa rcmp Historical Branch, for pointing me in the right direction and for casting his professional eye over the manuscript for accuracy in police references. Thanks to Rob Sanders, my publisher, and my editor, Jennifer Glossop, who has made another one better. Thanks to Byrna Barclay, who kept saying, "Not another letter!" and who gave me so much of her time, advice and encouragement, not to mention her office, computer and Kleenex for several days. Thanks to Moira Gilmour, who read the manuscript and made suggestions for the truth of the Scottish voice, customs and geographical references, and to Betty Graham, my test reader. Thanks to my old friend, June Gibson, for her generous support, and to friends and family for putting up with me these last two years. And very special thanks to Scott Simmie, who made sure I got to Scotland and home again.

All letters, police reports and telegrams are from the National Archives of Canada. I also consulted the following sources in the writing of this book:

Christina Stewart and Lynn Hudson. *Murder in Uniform*. Privately published, 1978.

Iain Somerville and Christine Warren. *Bygone Carluke*. Glasgow: Lanarkshire Heritage Series, 1991.

Ellen Pettigrew. *The Silent Enemy: Canada and the Deadly Flu of 1918*. Saskatoon: Western Producer Prairie Books, 1983.

René J. Dubois. *The White Plague*. New Brunswick, New Jersey: Rutgers University Press, 1987.

Mark Caldwell. *The Last Crusade: The War on Consumption 1862–1954*. New York: Athenium, 1988.

Patricia Giesler. *Valour Remembered: Canada and the First World War*. Ottawa: Department of Veteran Affairs, 1982.

The Saskatoon *Daily Star*, 1919–1920.

∾ CONTENTS ∾

✑ PROLOGUE ✐

Saskatchewan, 1918
In a dark office building on Scarth Street in Regina, a ninth-floor window is lit, as it often is these cold December nights. Superintendent Charles Augustus Mahony is working late. The second annual report of the Saskatchewan Provincial Police to the attorney general is due, and there is much to report: more than a thousand assaults, five hundred thefts, eight murders, the lists go on and on.

Gusts of icy wind buffet the building. Through a curtain of drifting snow, the light in the window burns on.

✑

In a shallow grave in a culvert near Waldheim, thirty miles from Saskatoon, lies the body of a young woman, almost six months pregnant. She is dressed in a blue tweed suit of fine-quality British wool, beautifully handmade, and a navy coat. On the shoulder of the suit, stained dark with blood, is the remnant of a corsage. She is wrapped in a coarse wool car robe.

As Charles Mahony works late in his Regina office, the December snows drift higher over the grave, which is somewhat protected from the sweep of freezing winds by the culvert. Now and then on the road above, a team of horses pulls muffled figures through the night on their way to or from Waldheim; an occasional Model T rattles and coughs its way to the city, perhaps for a medical emergency, perhaps piloted by a bachelor desperate for the sight of a human face, any place other than an isolated prairie shack with frost riming the cracks in the walls.

Apart from these passing disturbances, there are only the sounds of wind and drifting snow, the snapping of twigs in the frigid air, and, in the long, star-hung nights, a coyote's yelp, the soft hoot of an owl.

✑

The couple renting rooms at 217 9th Street in Saskatoon seem very much in love. They moved into the handsome rooming house on

October 1, and were often seen walking in the mellow fall evenings, or driving in a new Grey Dort. He wears the uniform of the Military Police, which suits his slim frame and craggy good looks. But to an astute observer, the marks of a recent illness are discernible: a certain pale fragility and the drawn, listening expression of one attuned to slight shifts from within. His young wife's solicitous manner supports this observation. They have eyes only for each other, though at times her loving glances find him deep in sombre thought.

Perhaps he is not well. There is reason for concern: the flu that ravaged Europe has arrived, the first cases reported in the east. Or perhaps he is just homesick for Scotland.

∾

The woman in the shallow grave knows no more loving glances. She will never see her home again.

∾

Charles Mahony is pleased with the fledgling police force he had so hastily assembled to begin law enforcement in January 1917. The attorney general's order to form a provincial force in just twenty-five days launched a mission that at the outset seemed nearly impossible. Mahony raided police forces across the country, and he had an eye for good prospects: he once saw two men laying bricks in Regina and hired them on the spot. And now Mahony has reason to feel proud of the record emerging from his Underwood typewriter: a chronicle of hundreds of minor offences and grievances discreetly but thoroughly handled and myriad patrols from ten to one hundred miles and more. Sometimes hundreds of miles are covered to investigate a death, only to find that the person died of natural causes.

∾

The woman under the culvert did not die of natural causes. No one is investigating her death.

∾

Mahony leans back and runs a hand over his bald head, his keen dark eyes looking beyond the green painted wall, cluttered with memos. The original raggle-taggle band, formed to relieve the enormity of the task facing the Royal North West Mounted Police, has grown to 106 men, sixty-two of whom are ex-Mounties and another twenty-four with experience in police forces throughout the world. A professional, proud force gaining the respect of the people.

They call him Manny at his suggestion because he hates being called Mahoney (no one pronounces it correctly—Mah-ha-ny) and he knows that behind his back the men affectionately call him Charles Augustus. The good reputation of this force is no small accomplishment, considering the population of the province is now 782,267, which averages out at one law enforcer for every 7,379 people. To say nothing of the logistics of covering so large a territory: 250,000 square miles.

And the population is still growing, a steady stream arriving from everywhere it seems; men with land in their eyes, entrepreneurial schemes in their heads. Some will succeed, some fail. And some will turn to crime. Nothing they do will surprise Charles Mahony much. In thirty years of police work, he has seen it all.

In the silent building the typewriter clatters on: cattle thefts, indecent assaults, arson, robbery, child neglect, murder.

∾

One murder is not recorded.

∾

The pile of papers on the oak desk is sizable; he is almost finished. Mahony gets up to stretch and look out the window. Smoke from the chimneys hangs in the frigid air, then dissipates momentarily with a gust of wind. A muffled figure leaning into the wind passes under a street light. A hard place, this Saskatchewan, and big enough to be a country. But interesting. Always that.

He returns to his chair, picks up the pile of papers and taps it on the desk to straighten it. A record of good men fulfilling their duties with courage and growing maturity. Other good men will be coming home from the war. He looks forward to finding some excellent recruits among their numbers. Whatever 1919 holds, it will not be dull. Of that he can be sure.

The job is done until next year. The light in the upstairs window goes out, and Charles Mahony heads home for a few hours of sleep.

BOOK ONE

There's a Wee Wifie Waiting

Chapter 1
∽ A GOOD MATCH ∾

Mary Hutchison, called Polly by her family and friends, was liked by everyone in the village of Slamannan in the Southern Uplands of Scotland, and loved by those who knew her well. She was small and slim with warm brown eyes and an abundance of shining brown hair.

Born in 1886 to a gentle, religious family, she grew up looking forward to a life much like that of her parents. Her father, William Hutchison, like most men in the village, worked as a coal miner. Financially unable to train for the ministry, his heart's desire, William was determined his children would fulfil their dreams. Three of Polly's sisters were teachers, her brother James attended university in Glasgow, and Polly and another sister trained as dressmakers. As a parish elder, William Hutchison was widely known and respected, and his wife Helen's generosity endeared her to everyone. The Hutchisons were poor but proud of their good name. Not a breath of scandal had ever touched any of them.

Even in this close family, Polly was special. "We all loved one another but somehow every one of us had a special work with Polly. She was so bright and cheery and brave," her sister Elizabeth would say later.

When Polly was eighteen, she went to work for Grossart Drapers in Carluke, where her brother Jim lived. Carluke was just twenty miles from Glasgow, in the heart of the Clyde Valley district. Mr. Grossart was a good employer, treating his staff like family, and among the job's other attractions was a slim, handsome young man who worked there as a draper. His name was John Wilson.

John's parents, well along in years before their children were born, owned a thriving grocery and grain business in Carluke. They were respected throughout the district as quiet, industrious, honest people. John was the second oldest of their four children. Like most people, he gravitated to Polly Hutchison; her sunny disposition complemented his moody, intense nature. A year after they met, he began to court her, and they fell in love.

The Hutchison family soon treated Jack, as he was called, as one of their own. Whomever Polly loved, they would love. And Wilson's family became fond of Polly. When Jack requested her hand in marriage in August 1906, all were pleased—and a bit relieved after Jack's dramatic announcement that if Polly wasn't allowed to marry him he would blow his brains out. The level-headed Hutchisons did not believe anyone would be so irrational. They did not yet know John Wilson.

Jack presented Polly with "a nice little diamond ring." Their courtship wasn't rushed. They had known each other four years, courting for three of them, before they married on January 1, 1908. The young couple spent their honeymoon in Dublin.

Soon after the wedding, Jack Wilson's parents both died, leaving some money to him and some to his twin sisters, Mary and Isabella. Through the Scottish law of primogeniture, the oldest son, Alex, inherited the bulk of the estate, including the business in Carluke.

Jack quit his job at Grossart and, in partnership with Polly's brother James, invested in several greenhouses. The gentle slopes of the Clyde Valley were perfect for gardening. Jack, who had suffered from lung trouble since childhood, found the greenhouses' humidity stifling, and he worked outdoors as much as possible. He and Polly moved into a lovely old stone house, part of Jack's father's estate, in Kilncadzow (pronounced Kilkeggie by the locals), three miles from Carluke. They were off to a fine start in life.

Everyone agreed it was a good match. Jack Wilson was crazy about his "wee wifie," and the Wilsons were an affectionate, popular couple, with a close circle of friends. Polly's family noticed Jack's tendency to lie when it suited his purposes, but Polly seemed oblivious to it.

In May 1909, a son, George, was born, and Polly had what she wanted in life: a home and family. Wilson was a good father. As soon as he could walk, the boy was his constant companion, following his father everywhere, "helping" with the chores. Everyone commented on the close bond between father and son and on how good Jack was with the "wean."

An idyllic life, it would seem, but not for long.

Chapter II
∽ GEOGRAPHIC CURE ∾

Alex Wilson's heart was not in the grocery trade, and in a very few years his neglect and indifference ran his parents' once-thriving business into the ground.

"Pure laziness and nothing else," Jim Hutchison told his sister Polly. "That was a good, solid business."

In his sudden frantic attempts to salvage the business, Alex talked his sister Mary out of two hundred pounds, and he raised a further three hundred by granting a bond on the property. Then he forged the signature of an old friend of his father's, who had left his bankbook in George Wilson's honest hands for deposits. When George died, Mrs. Wilson took over that duty, and Alex agreed to do it when his mother died. Alex stole five hundred pounds.

Jack, who couldn't bear to see the once-respected business end in disgrace, took money out of the greenhouse business to pay off his brother's debts. When things continued to slide, he panicked and stole money outright from his brother-in-law, Jim Hutchison, to pay creditors. All to no avail. When the bank foreclosed in October 1911, the Wilson family business brought Alex twenty-eight pounds.

When people learned of the measures the brothers had taken, they were scandalized. Alex's stealing from a trusting old man was seen as despicable, as was Jack's taking money from his wife's family. The Wilsons' good reputation lay in ruins, and Jack felt humiliated and disgraced. He never forgave Alex.

Polly's family protected her from the worst of the scandal. Over cups of tea in his cluttered greenhouse office, Jim Hutchison vented his feelings to his sister Elizabeth. Elizabeth taught school in the district, and her fiancé, Archie Craig, had bought a partnership in the greenhouses. He was living with Jack and Polly till his marriage in August 1912.

"Liars, Jack and Alex both," Jim said.

"They must have been feeling desperate." Elizabeth, like Polly, always tried to see the best in people.

Jim snorted. "Do you realize Jack's bankrupted the gardens? That makes me a desperate man. Should I go out then and steal from some helpless old man?"

"I know, but Jack is our brother-in-law."

"More's the pity. Everybody knows Alex is crooked as a dog's hind leg, but I never thought it of Jack." Jim leaned over to pick some spent blossoms from a potted plant on his desk. "Did you know he's thinking of running away to Canada? I'd say good riddance if it wasn't for the bairn and the one on the way."

"Archie told me that. But surely Jack won't go and leave Polly. Not in her condition."

"No, I suppose not."

But Jack Wilson had indeed developed an urge to travel. Swayed by the propaganda luring emigrants to the Canadian prairies, he bought a ticket to Saskatoon in the province of Saskatchewan. He would sail in July 1912.

"He could have stayed and faced it," his sister Mary told Polly. "The rest of us did." Of course, Jack could have told Mary it's easier to face the music if you aren't the one who wrote it.

Polly was six months pregnant when he left.

"It's only for a year," he told her, kissing her again and again. "Alex will straighten things out and I'll be back."

"Daddy, please don't go!" Little George, who followed him everywhere, clung to his leg. "Please, Daddy!"

Archie Craig, waiting to take Jack to the train for Liverpool, stepped outside to give them privacy. Through the window he heard the boy crying as if his heart would break. Archie heartily wished Jack would hurry up; they were in danger of missing the train, and he just made it harder for everybody this way.

Finally Jack emerged and climbed in the trap.

"I'll be back in a year," he called. "I'll write lots of letters."

At the station, Jack gripped Archie's hand.

"Promise me, Archie, that you will look after Polly and be good to her for my sake."

"You have my word, Jack."

"My wee lassie is all the world to me," Jack said, with tears in his eyes. There was a lot of the actor in Jack Wilson. Like many Scots, he went through life "treading God's boards."

So a shamed and aggrieved Jack Wilson left his quiet village in the pastoral Clyde Valley. In Liverpool, he boarded a steamer headed for Canada. Standing on the crowded deck as the steamer pulled away from the overflowing dock, he heard a wistful sound drifting over the water. "Should auld acquaintance be forgot, and never brought to mind," sang those left behind, in the tradition of the time, waving hundreds of damp handkerchiefs in the summer air. This plaintive acknowledgement that auld acquaintance can indeed be forgotten was followed by much cheering as the ship gathered speed.

Wilson shared a cabin seven feet square with upper and lower bunks on three sides and the door on the fourth, all below the water line. In the words of one 1913 passenger: "The grub was dished up in washtubs and you helped yourself. It took twelve days to make the crossing, and I want to tell you the North Atlantic is no place to be in April." Since there was no privacy with two thousand people jammed together, Wilson spent most of his time on deck, where the air was fresh.

It would have been hard for passengers not to think of the fate of the "unsinkable" liner, *Titanic*, which had sunk a few days out of Southampton on her maiden voyage just two months before. But Wilson's crossing was uneventful.

In Halifax, Nova Scotia, Wilson transferred to a westbound train crowded with immigrants from all over Great Britain and Europe. Some were leaving from eastern Canada, too, where unemployment figures were rising.

Most came hoping for a better life, the chance to own some land. Some, like Wilson, were fleeing scandals at home, and many would never look back. If a man was too well dressed, he was suspected of being a remittance man—one of the alcoholics and ne'er-do-wells, paid by well-to-do families to stay away.

Observing the Poles, Germans and Ukrainians sharing his journey, Wilson would have been shocked (but, as a Scot, secretly pleased) to learn that English labourers were among the least favoured immigrants. Employers complained that they often brought trade union ideas with them. Soon after Wilson's arrival, the years of prosperity ended, and long lines of men applying for work were greeted with signs flatly stating, "English Need Not Apply."

The train compartments were large compared to those on British trains. In pull-down overhead bunks bare of mattresses, women prepared for bed behind pinned-up blankets and newspapers. At the end of each coach was a small compartment with a stove for heating food, and men's and women's washrooms. The smells of ethnic foods mingled and drifted out into the coach as faces from many countries peered through the grimy windows at the immensity and variety of this new land.

Day after night after day they rocked along, through thick spruce forests with glimpses of rocky coastline, past apple orchards, the stares of grazing cows, great rushing unpolluted rivers, virgin hardwood forests, clear lakes, verdant valleys, and the marvellous St. Lawrence River. Gentle, rolling Ontario gradually levelled out as the train rocked westward and the prairies unfolded. So much land. So much sky. So few people.

The ships were packed; the trains crowded; and settlers' belongings piled high on every station platform. The next year, 1913, the number of immigrants to Canada would reach an all-time record of 400,870.

Wilson wrote letter after letter to Polly as he travelled west. His long, newsy, often passionate letters described what he saw and assured her they'd be separated no more than a year. It was Alex's fault for making him an exile. Polly kept every letter

Chapter III

THE EIGHT-YEAR-OLD WONDER OF THE BRITISH EMPIRE

And why did John Wilson choose Saskatoon as his destination? He was one of the many enchanted by the rhetoric that shamelessly billed that faraway prairie city as "The Fastest Growing City in the World," "The Minneapolis & St. Paul of the West" and "The Eight-Year-Old Wonder of the British Empire." At Canadian emigration offices in

London, Edinburgh and elsewhere in the United Kingdom, crowds pressed around the windows to see working models of Saskatchewan grain elevators and to read about the wonders of the Canadian prairies. Large signs announced "160 Acre Farms in Western Canada, Free, Improved Farms at Reasonable Prices, Healthy Climate" (no mention of 50-degree-below-zero winters), and so on. The Canadian Emigration Office in London faced Trafalgar Square, and the 1904 Department of Interior report stated: "The bright and attractive nature of the [Emigration Office] buildings will be emblematic to many of the bright future which Canada has to offer." The people of Great Britain were being courted, and they capitulated by the thousands.

There was at least some substance behind the rhetoric. Saskatoon was indeed a burgeoning city, ringing with the sounds of hammers and saws and the shouts and laughter of men, and imbued with the smells of sawdust, horse manure and money. Horses and a few cars crowded the city streets, and the bustle of commerce was everywhere.

New cement sidewalks appeared overnight. Dirt flew from scores of shovels as miles of trenches were dug and sewer pipe laid, and the tracks for the new street railway gleamed between the horse droppings. Saskatoon had nine architectural firms, twelve automobile dealers, sixteen livery stables, thirteen banks, fourteen poolrooms, five employment offices, nine theatres and two massage parlours. The handsome stone buildings of the university were rising on the high south bank of the river.

The city sprawled on both sides of the pristine South Saskatchewan River—hence the Minneapolis/St. Paul comparison—already spanned by a traffic bridge on Victoria Avenue and a railroad bridge farther east. Saskatoon looked just like a city. All it needed were more people. A fierce rivalry for citizens had sprung up between Saskatoon and Regina, the capital city. The city fathers wrote ever more alluring propaganda to attract settlers, and on census days they counted every live body they found, including transients and those passed out by the railway tracks. And prairie boosterism was perceived to be the duty of all good citizens. Some lonely prairie homemakers, living in sod shacks, must have laughed behind their aprons. Or cried.

It is highly unlikely that Wilson's train arrived on time. Trains into Saskatoon rarely arrived on schedule; so rarely that a train that did earned this account in a 1903 *Saskatoon Phenix* (which later became the *Saskatoon Phoenix*, the *Saskatoon Star Phoenix*, and finally the *Star Phoenix*):

> The southbound train from Prince Albert was on time on Tuesday morning, December 30, to the amazement and consternation of the citizens. Letters were unwritten, passengers were still in bed. Visitors called their hosts to the door to see the unique spectacle, and mothers impressed it upon their children as a never-to-be-forgotten occurrence. Newly married couples who set their dates in the hope of a train behind time were politely left behind and lovers who came away from home expecting to return by a "behind time" train had to look for lodging. What a little thing it takes to set all the machinery of society in confusion. When will it happen again? The *Phenix* one year free to the first person who guesses the correct date up to April 1st, 1903.

Almost immediately, Wilson was hired onto a bridge and building crew, one of the many working long hours to keep up with the demand. He first worked on the University Bridge, which would not be completed until 1916. At lunchtime, with the clamour of hammers on iron silent, the men watched fish jumping in the clear river that curved in both directions. As they sat and smoked with legs dangling over the side, they had a perfect view of the changing autumn colours and the burgeoning city on both sides of the river.

Good housing had become scarce and expensive, but Wilson managed to find lodging in a rooming house. He did not mix much, and every Sunday he faithfully wrote to Polly: long, newsy, often ardent letters, which Polly read over and over. During this period he also dutifully sent home quite a lot of money.

Chapter IV

ᔋ POOR JACK ᔌ

At the butcher's, Polly bought lamb for stew, then stopped at Grossart Drapers for white silk thread and seam binding for Elizabeth's wedding dress. It was almost finished, and Lizzie looked lovely in it. Polly wished Jack could be there for the wedding. Well, she would just have a good time without him. All their family and friends were coming and it would be wonderful. Except that people didn't know what to say about Jack and that made it a bit uncomfortable sometimes. They didn't think it was right, his going to Canada and leaving her. Indeed, some of them were quite outspoken about it.

Well, it would pass; slowly, to be sure, but it would pass. And if they thought he didn't care enough for her, she wished they could see his letters. On second thought it was a good thing they couldn't. Really, he shouldn't say such things on paper!

She walked over to Chapel Street to buy a can of Ensign tea at Johnny Morton's grocery shop.

It was a beautiful day. She would have liked to walk up to the top of Windmill Brae, one of her favourite places even in winter when the wind swept cold and wet over the Bashaw Moor (the BashyMeer, they called it). If you ran down towards the moor you felt as if you might suddenly take wing. She'd earn herself a look or two if she did that now, almost eight months' pregnant. As she smiled at the thought, the new bairn gave her a healthy kick under the ribcage.

The Tinto Hill was lovely today, just emerging through a veil of blue. The approaching sunlight, moving across the land revealed bit by bit the hills and fields and vales between that grand hill and the village. Like God creating the earth. The whole Thomson family was out picking strawberries in their garden as she passed down the road. Annie Thomson looked up and waved. They had planted the berries front and back this year, Polly saw. Many people, including herself, grew strawberries to sell to the jam factory. Well, she mustn't dawdle because Lizzie was looking after wee George. What would she do without her sister? They'd become closer than ever since Jack left.

Polly gratefully accepted when Alex McKay stopped and offered her a ride most of the way home.

Elizabeth, with her nephew in her arms, watched from the window as Polly came down the road. He'd just got up from his nap, and he leaned into her, still heavy with sleep. As Polly passed under the kitchen window, Elizabeth saw the letter poking out from her sister's bag.

"Here's Mammy," she said, putting the boy down to run and greet Polly. Elizabeth put the kettle on to boil.

As soon as they were settled at the table with tea and the bairn on his mother's lap—he hated to let her out of his sight since Jack left—Polly read the letter.

"Oh, dear. How terrible! Listen to this. 'Well, Polly, you won't believe the things that happen here. In Regina, that's 150 miles from here, there was a terrible cyclone yesterday. It came out of nowhere and flattened blocks and blocks of buildings, and they think 65 people were killed. One man was in the tub when it hit and the wall of his house blew out and he went sailing through the air scrubbing his back.' "

At this the little boy laughed. The women, too. " 'Three churches were hit, all brand new, one was completely wrecked, I think it was the Methodist. It makes you wonder. And from what they're telling me about the winters here, maybe a cyclone isn't the worst. I think they exaggerate for us green fellows, they like to rib us . . . ' " Polly folded the letter. She would read the rest later.

"Poor Jack. What a terrible, hard country," she said, getting up and stoking the fire. "Who would want to live there? Cyclones and terrible thunderstorms, and those awful winters. Oh, I'll be so glad when he's home again."

Elizabeth didn't answer. Polly knew how she felt about Jack going, even if she didn't say so.

Polly cubed the lamb, salted and peppered it and dropped it in the sizzling pot with a bay leaf and a leek. Polly's movements, always so quick, were slower and heavier now. She stopped to rub the small of her back as the good smell of browning meat filled the room.

"But, never mind, we've no time for gloomy thoughts. There's going to be a wedding soon. You must try the dress on, Lizzie, and let me have another look. Those tucks aren't sitting quite right."

Elizabeth carefully lifted down the white silk dress that hung in the bedroom doorway.

"And who's the lovely dress shirt on your sewing machine for? Is it Father's?" she asked.

"No, that one's for the Joiner." The Joiner was John's old uncle who'd been living with Polly and the boy ever since his house burned down. Polly had given him his dinner every day since she returned from her honeymoon, and she was glad of his company now that Jack was gone. He contributed a little, and he helped with the chores.

"Oh, but won't he be a splendid sight!" Elizabeth laughed and went to try on the dress, the fluttering silk skirt brushing the sides of the bedroom doorway.

Polly smiled after her sister, happy for her; Archie was a good man. And Polly was glad, too, for the distraction. Whatever the future held, they had a wedding to prepare for.

∞

In October, John and Polly Wilson's second child was born, a girl. Polly nearly died when she was born, perhaps of puerperal (childbed) fever, always a danger in the days before antibiotics.

Polly christened the little girl Helen after her grandmother, and they called her Ella to avoid confusion.

If Polly hoped the news that he had a daughter would bring Jack home, she was disappointed. He said when he left it would take a year for people to forget the fiasco, and nothing was going to take him back sooner.

Chapter v

∽ HARD LUCK ∾

And so Jack Wilson experienced his first prairie winter. A hard one. He was laid off his bridge-building job in the spring, and found work as a gardener in Saskatoon's new parks.

In the fall of 1914, falling wages (labourers had yet to organize a successful union), high living costs and the acute housing shortage prompted him to move to Prince Albert, where he planned to start a tomato-growing business. No doubt he hoped to emulate the successful market gardens in the Clyde Valley. But at Prince Albert, ninety miles northeast of Saskatoon in heavily wooded spruce and pine country, the growing season is extremely short. And the moderate, gentle growing conditions of Scotland are not the ways of Saskatchewan.

On a muggy afternoon in July 1914, a black sky overlaid with billowing ochre-white clouds rolled over the garden and cabin in the clearing, and then he heard a sudden, shocking clamour of hailstones banging the roof and rattling down the tin chimney. Jack watched in disbelief from the doorway of his one-roomed shack as huge hailstones leapt and danced crazily among the rows and rows of tomato plants, pounding his hopes as flat as the crop.

He stood among the ruined plants, shaking his fist at the sky as the clouds passed over, uncovering a watery sun. All the outdoor work in the last two years had given him a deceptively healthy glow, and he'd put some muscle on his slim frame since he left home, but his expression was bleak. Once again, things had gone wrong for Jack Wilson.

He had hardly written to Polly since leaving Saskatoon, and not to any of his family for more than a year. He felt disconnected from the old country and everyone in it. But what did he have here? A shack with a stove, a bed, a table, a chair and a half acre of tomato sauce. He couldn't take a winter in this place. His lungs would never stand it.

Nor were the prospects good anywhere he could see. The incredible building boom had already burst with the collapse of railway construction in 1913, the inevitable result of too many railways and too much building too fast. What with rising prices and a three-year drought, the downturn was sudden and hard, leaving thousands, like himself, unemployed. In the railway centre of Moose Jaw, Jack knew, the soup kitchen lines stretched for blocks. It would be the same everywhere. In the east, lines of men waited at the railway freight sheds, shipyards, anywhere they might get a few hours' work. There was no welfare, no relief, and men coming west looking for work found more of the same.

Jack could see only one solution. War in Europe seemed inevitable, and joining up would provide him with a ticket back overseas. He didn't relish going back with his tail between his legs, nor did he want to go to war, but enlisting would be a way to get back without losing face. The only way, really. If it came, he would go.

∾

War was declared on August 4, 1914, when Jack Wilson was working on a neighbouring farm. Britain's ultimatum to Germany demanding its withdrawal from Belgium expired, and the British Empire, including Canada, was at war.

Canada was no reluctant warrior. Young men couldn't join up fast enough. If everyone said it was a just cause, then it must be so. And if your country thought you were worth a $1.10 a day, so much the better. In those delirious early days, there was no need for conscription. That would come later. All the pundits of the time were predicting a short, decisive war. If massed armies didn't settle the issue quickly, economic collapse surely would. Men swarmed to the recruiting offices, afraid the war would be over before they could get there. From farms and small communities all over the west they came, by any means available. One young Englishman homesteading near Rosetown walked eighty miles to Saskatoon in his "well-ventilated overalls" to enlist. Exultant patriotic demonstrations erupted, and just ten days after war was declared, Saskatoon cheered its first volunteers on their way. With bands playing and flags waving, the crowd at the Canadian Pacific Railway depot was so thick the men had difficulty boarding, and their train was delayed an hour.

In the east, excitement soared even higher. The country went mad. People were singing in the streets and roads. Everybody wanted to be a hero. According to one veteran:

> I wanted to be a hero too, but I wasn't big enough, five foot nothing and weighed 85 pounds and was a Boy Scout bugler . . . I was nineteen, but looked fifteen . . . I was sworn in, tested, inoculated and in half an hour I'm in the army. I lay awake all night thinking *What have I done?* And I went away in my first suit. I paid a dollar for it and it almost fell off me.

When asked what the training was like, he laughed.

Oh God, what training? The training amounted to being equipped with the old South African equipment. Some of it was mouldy—a leather bag, a haversack, a water bottle and the Ross rifle. What a bastard! Germans coming on in mass, and the rifle wouldn't fire, the bolt wouldn't close, the steel wasn't tempered. They'd try to drive it open and they'd blow their brains out.

In early October, 32,000 ill-trained soldiers left for England.

As soon as he heard war was declared, John Wilson headed for Prince Albert to enlist, but was rejected because of his weak lungs.

Two weeks later, while walking down Main Street in Prince Albert, a poster on the side of the livery stable caught his eye. The Royal North West Mounted Police were looking for recruits. There were certain requirements—literacy, height and so on, which he fulfilled. He went straight to their Prince Albert detachment to inquire about enlisting. They sent him to their doctor for an examination, and he passed. Although it's unlikely his health had improved dramatically in two weeks, the problem apparently didn't render him unfit for the Mounties. In August 1914, the month Wilson joined, the RNWMP, in anticipation of difficulties with the large foreign-born population in the west, increased the size of the force by five hundred men. With so many of their men joining the armed forces when their term was up, the RNWMP was desperately in need of recruits.

The war was only one of the reasons for a mass exodus of men from the ranks of the Mounted Police. Almost no one whose term expired in 1914 and early 1915 re-engaged with the force; most joined the war effort and headed overseas. The dismally low wages, poor housing and daunting workload were also factors: men were expected to be on duty twenty-four hours a day, seven days a week, for low wages—sixty cents a day for new men, and a dollar a day after eight years' service— the same as was paid elsewhere for unskilled labour. By the time Wilson joined, the force was manned largely by new arrivals from the United Kingdom, lured by recruiting officers and the publicity that painted such a romantic picture of the men in scarlet.

Jack Wilson, however, was grateful for the reprieve. He arrived at Depot Division, Regina, for training. At the age of thirty, he had a new chance in life. He resolved to excel as an officer of the law.

Chapter VI

∽ NEWS ∼

To Polly Wilson, as to many others, events were spiralling out of control. One might think that nothing in her life had prepared her for living daily with fear and uncertainty, and yet everything in her life had prepared her for it. Her strong religious upbringing had instilled in her an unshakable faith in God, and she needed it now. As she needed the cheerful, optimistic nature she was born with. Jack's letters, which had once arrived weekly and sometimes more often, were now few and far between. Months apart, sometimes. And the children were growing so fast. It made her sad to think he'd never seen little Ella, who was running all over. And George didn't ask about his father so much any more.

"Has he sent you any money lately?" asked Elizabeth, who came by every day after school.

"As much as he could manage, I'm sure."

This meant precious little. Or none.

It was easier for Elizabeth to visit since Polly needed every minute she could spare from the children for sewing. Something was always in progress on her sewing machine in the corner.

"As soon as the war is over, he'll be home, I know," Polly said.

"That might be a long time," Elizabeth said, then, seeing the look on her sister's face, said, "What's that you're sewing now, Polly? Isn't it a beautiful colour? Just like a peacock's feather."

"Yes, isn't it? It's Margaret Stewart's wedding dress."

"Oh, won't she be lovely in that colour? Most of the girls aren't bothering with wedding dresses, are they, with so many boys going to France?"

"No, thank goodness, I can hardly keep up now, along with the piecework Mr. Grossart sends me, bless his kind heart." Polly got up and took a johnnycake from the stove. It made Elizabeth sad to see how thin and tired she looked. "People have been so good to me, Lizzie."

"Doesn't Father always say we reap what we sow? It's just your turn to reap, that's all."

The kitchen door opened, and the Joiner came in, stamping his feet on the mat. He grinned at Elizabeth and Polly, and wiped an arthritic hand over his wet, white hair.

"Mmm. Something smells good."

Jack's two sisters had offered to take him in after his house burned but his answer was, "Nae, I'll just gang awa' wi' Polly." The old carpenter had presented her with his most prized possession; his stuffed, only slightly singed pet fox. It stood on the hearth with one paw lifted, its head turned and its spiteful, beady eyes fixed on whatever was going on in the room. The dog's hair stood on end and he growled every time he caught sight of it, to the Joiner's great amusement.

He hung his jacket by the back door and placed his rubber boots neatly under it.

"By the Lord Harry, that's a cold rain out there." Then with a little smile at Polly he pulled a letter from under his sweater. "There you go, lassie, a letter from your Johnny. And speakin' of Johnny . . ."

Elizabeth laughed and cut the cake. Polly, hungry for word from Jack, was already lost in the letter.

"Oh, listen to Jack's news," she cried. " 'I tried to join up but the doctor said my lungs don't sound so good and they turned me down. Then I heard that the Mounties were wanting men so I applied and they accepted me! Now what do you think of that, Polly, your Jack boy a mounted policeman! I'll be training here in Regina and then they'll send me out to a detachment. I thought I could ride a horse till I got here, but they're pleased at my marksmanship.

" 'They won't pay much but you'll be getting a separation allowance every month and I'll send you as much as I can. At least I'll get food and lodging and a bed (I *hope*—the place is overflowing with recruits and they ran out of mattresses so I sleep on bare boards with just a wee bit of padding), but it's steady work and people really look up to the Mounties here. I hear they'll be sending a cavalry unit overseas, so maybe you'll see me sooner than you think.' "

Polly looked at the Joiner and Elizabeth for reassurance. "His lungs can't be too bad, can they, if they took him in the police force? My, won't he look handsome in a Mountie's uniform?"

Polly's step was lighter as she went to get the children from their afternoon nap.

Chapter VII

ᘯ BLAINE LAKE ᘰ

In the town of Blaine Lake, everyone noticed the new policeman who arrived in July 1915. Jack Wilson cut a striking figure in the RNWMP uniform.

His training had been intensive, months of foot drill, physical training, self-defence, small arms, explosives, first aid, riot control, prohibition maintainence and police-community relations. And every aspect of horsemanship had been practised over and over till man and horse were one.

And finally graduation. Wilson had proudly recited the oath: "I will faithfully, diligently, and impartially execute and perform my duties in the Royal North West Mounted Police Force, without fear, favour, or affection of or towards any person or party, so help me God."

And his reward for all that hard work: a badge pinned to his tunic, inscribed with the motto of the force: *Maintien Le Droit*, Uphold the Right. And that was exactly what he intended to do.

The duties of his new job took him away from Blaine Lake on a variety of missions: scouting for stills and on "lunatic detail"—the apprehension and transportation of the insane to the Saskatchewan Hospital at North Battleford. He also followed up every lead on the activities of suspected enemy aliens, often only to find that someone with a grievance had tried to make trouble for his immigrant neighbour. Many of these people were suspect simply because of their surnames.

A colony of Dukobors had settled in the Blaine Lake area, and keeping a watch on their activities was a primary responsibility of the local Mountie. He tried to get along with them, since when they were displeased with his interference—such as his insistence that they send their children to school—they flung off all their clothes, no matter what the temperature or circumstances, and sometimes set things on fire.

In Blaine Lake, Corporal Wilson was housed in a small building on Main Street, which the town council had purchased for the purpose. The accommodation must have been considered inadequate since the secretary wrote the district office in Prince Albert about the possibility of "new quarters for the Mounted Police." Councilors were instructed to interview Dr. Borgeault about purchasing his house for police purposes, but apparently the good doctor didn't wish to part with it.

Blaine Lake was a vigorous, forward-looking town, serving a large area between Saskatoon and Prince Albert. It boasted a large hotel, a bank, a school, three livery stables, a pharmacy, two cafés, a pool hall, an implement dealer, a lumberyard and other businesses. Two dance halls often held rival dances on Saturday nights, while stores and businesses stayed open until 11:00 P.M. to accommodate farmers. The downtown wooden sidewalks were a constant headache for council, with horsedrawn vehicles always breaking the crossings down, and hitching post rings in the sidewalks impeding foot traffic.

Other new arrivals in Blaine Lake in 1915 included John and Allison Patterson, farmers who moved there with their four children: Mac, James, Jessie and Kate.

John Patterson purchased the livery stable owned by R. B. (Byron) Horner. One of Saskatchewan's most colourful figures, Horner had come west from Quebec on a harvest excursion in 1906 and settled in the area. At the age of twenty-three, he began to import breeding horses from the large horse farms in the east, spending most of his winters travelling between Saskatchewan and Quebec, bringing back carloads of horses. "It took two weeks to make the journey one way," he said. "I was always on the train in those days." The return fare from Saskatoon to Shawville, Quebec, was about seventeen dollars. Travelling with R. B. and the horses was a ticket to adventure for many young men from both provinces, and the arrivals by train of these spirited purebred horses were exciting events.

Horner later went into politics, eventually becoming the first director for Saskatchewan of the Canadian National Railway, and a senator.

The Pattersons' house was next door to the barn where Jack Wilson stabled his horse. In the summer of 1916, John Patterson, an affable man, invited the new Mountie home for supper, and there he met Jessie, a willowy sixteen-year-old with a lovely high-cheekboned face and thick brown hair. Gradually their house became the place he gravitated to when he had time to spare, and an extra place was often set at their table when Jack returned from his excursions into the countryside.

He was grateful for the Pattersons' kindness. His spartan accommodation did not feel much like a home, and the job was a lonely one. Mounties were forbidden to speak to the public about their work or the workings of the RNWMP in general, and this secretiveness, while adding to their mystique, isolated its members. This policy earned the Northwesters the title the Silent Force. Wilson also said nothing about his wife and children back in Scotland. People in Blaine Lake, including the Pattersons, assumed he was single, and he didn't set the record straight. His other life seemed very remote.

It was now more than four years since he had left Scotland, and Jack Wilson's letters home had slowed to a trickle. He felt he had done all he could to get back home. He had tried to enlist to get back to the old country. His hope that he'd be sent overseas with the Mounties was dimming, and on his wages he'd never be able to bring his family to Canada. But he had tried. Hadn't he always tried? Things just seemed to go against him.

But, after feeling like a failure, he had found something he was good at, something with a certain cachet; people looked up to him.

Wilson was not the only lawman in the area. S. D. Jones, the first town constable, had been hired in 1912 at fifteen dollars a month to maintain law and order in the village. It's to be hoped there was not much lawlessness and disorder in Blaine Lake since Jones's other duties included repairing sidewalks and crossings, collecting poll and dog taxes, the collection and payment of licences, inspection of weeds, maintainence of water pumps and fire apparatus, ringing the curfew bell three times a day, inspecting buildings, enforcing the pound bylaw, taking care of street lamps, putting in hitching posts, collecting and recharging fire extinguishers, inspecting sanitary conditions and planting peonies in the schoolyard. Although the local Mountie was in charge of the rural area rather than the village, his presence did help to keep law and order. S. D. Jones must have been grateful.

At the time of Wilson's arrival, Blaine Lake was not a "dry" town. In July 1911, the village had passed a bylaw prohibiting the sale of intoxicating liquors, which resulted in tragedy in November 1912. Three men working on the railway grade stabled their horses, then bought a bottle of alcohol. Told the men wanted it for rubbing down horses, the druggist gave them wood alcohol, which the men promptly drank. Two died in the livery barn, and another was found in a granary a few miles away. He had choked trying to cool his throat and stomach with a mouthful of grain. In December 1913, a vote repealing the bylaw passed 185 to 5.

Although it wasn't a crime to drink liquor, it was against the law to make it, but many did, in stills hidden in the hilly, heavily wooded areas around Blaine Lake. Wilson, snooping around on his black horse or on foot, became an unwelcome and all-too-familiar sight.

After fulfilling his disparate duties, Jack found himself gravitating to the Pattersons' house and to Jessie. More and more often at those rival Saturday night dances, Jessie looked over the shoulder of a dance partner to where a uniformed Jack Wilson stood at the back of the hall. His feelings for her—their feelings for each other—were becoming serious.

In 1916, Wilson tried for a second time to enlist. He was rejected again. Later he would say that he had wished to leave for Jessie's sake, but it was also about this time that talk surfaced in Blaine Lake that Wilson was a married man. Given his record of running away from self-made predicaments, his motive may not have been entirely selfless.

Chapter VIII

✒ OVER THERE ✑

The war Wilson tried to get to had very early become a war of attrition. By autumn 1914, a military deadlock had been reached on both the eastern and western fronts, with opposing armies dug into deep trenches in the hard clay. These they fortified with everything they could find, thick tangled barbed wire, boulders, sandbags, mortar batteries and machine-gun nests. Backed up by support lines and heavy artillery, the men in the trenches faced the open space of no man's land. And, beyond that, the enemy.

By the time the war ended, the labyrinthine network of trenches would stretch all the way from the Belgian coast to Switzerland, a distance of more than six hundred miles. On this western front, Canadians fought and died by the tens of thousands.

That first contingent made up the largest convoy of men, horses and equipment ever to cross the Atlantic. The convoy included a regiment from the still-separate British Dominion of Newfoundland. After a winter training on the Salisbury Plain, the men were keen for battle, desperate to escape the cold, unrelenting drizzle on that sodden English plain. They didn't know what lay ahead.

At the second Battle of Ypres and St. Julien, the Germans unleashed poison gas. The Canadians, violently ill, gasping for air through mud-soaked handkerchiefs and struggling with jammed Ross rifles, held the line against all odds until fresh troops arrived. The cost was horrendous. In those forty-eight hours, 6,035 Canadians, one man in every three, was lost from Canada's small force of poorly trained men. And, in the days and years ahead, worse was to come. In one horrific battle, the Somme offensive (called *das Blutbad*—the blood bath—by the Germans), the 1st Newfoundland Regiment was virtually annihilated in less than half an hour. In one day 57,500 British and Canadians were killed, wounded or missing.

Apart from sending its young men off to the horrors of war, Saskatchewan saw its main role in the war effort as that of food provider. The war had ended the depression in agriculture. With huge armies in the trenches, the government needed all Canada could produce, and employers and farmers soon regretted that so many men had been encouraged to enlist. The demand drove prices up, and the wisdom that might have left the dry land of the Palliser Triangle to grazing was abandoned in favour of wheat-growing. The government, desperate for wheat, encouraged unsound farming practices, such as growing crops on stubble land.

The war and its consequent labour shortage changed many other things, also. The Imperial Munitions Board employed 250,000 Canadians, among them 40,000 women. Women's lives were changing.

Polly Wilson's life, however, was in limbo. In that windy, rainy Scottish village, another year had gone by with her husband still away. His letters had stopped, and no one in his family had heard from him since the beginning of the war. Polly feared greatly for her husband's health. He was not well, he'd said in his last letter, his lungs again.

Hurrying down the long windy road to Carluke with more piecework for Mr. Grossart flapping in her arms, she thought about Jack. Such strange work he had to do, taking madmen and women to that hospital for the insane. Sometimes they were dangerous. And he'd been bitten and kicked trying to put clothes back on those crazy Russian people. What were they called? Dukobors? Polly thought she'd never heard anything so strange as those large people who wanted to run around naked and set fire to things. It seemed as if a lot of people over there were going mad. Well, wasn't the whole world, when you thought about it?

She certainly wasn't alone. Whenever she started feeling sorry for herself, she had only to look at the black armbands, at the anguish and heartache on the faces of mothers, fathers, wives. And children, too, since so many married men were going now. Margaret Stewart, who hadn't been wed long enough to get used to calling herself by her married name, was a widow with a bairn to raise on her own.

And so many returned men would never be the same. Polly had written to Jack about William Angus, who was wounded forty times as he crawled into no man's land to rescue his friend, James Martin. Jack had grown up with both these men. Watching poor William receive his Victoria Cross had made her so sad. He seemed not to even know what all the crowd and cheering were about.

Polly passed a shop with a black ribboned wreath on the door. It was madness, the men of the world lining up to kill each other. And the *Lusitania*. She couldn't forget those heartbreaking pictures in the paper—one of a bairn about Ella's age, washed up on the shore in his wee Lord Fauntleroy suit. Sister Mary Buchanan from Slamannan, who at twenty-six was just three years younger than Polly, went down with the *Lusitania* on her way to Red Cross nursing duty in France. Just imagine, that great ship torpedoed and gone in twenty minutes, twelve hundred civilians drowning! It didn't bear thinking about. And the kaiser declaring a holiday and Germans dancing in the streets! Perhaps it was just as well Jack was safe in Canada.

If only he was well. If only he would write.

The wind tore at her clothes and hair, pulling at the garments she carried in her arms. As the first drops of rain spotted the cobblestones, she hurried her steps. She musn't get the clothes wet; the big umbrella she carried would be useless in this wind.

Polly tapped on the window at Grossart Drapers, and Mr. Grossart hurried to open the door for her, taking some of the clothing from her arms.

"Ah, Polly, you're a wonder. How would I get along without you?"

"I suspect better than I would without you and the work you give me out of the kindness of your heart," Polly said, laying the things out on the big work table in the back and starting to hang them up.

"Nonsense, my dear. You turn the finest seam in the county and you know it." Mr. Grossart took her pay envelope from under the tray in the cash register. "And have you heard—?"

She shook her head. "And what have you got for me this week?" she asked brightly.

Soon their heads were bent over the new work.

Chapter IX

∽ BAD NEWS ∾

As the war raged on, Jack Wilson was fighting a battle of his own. For months he had felt unwell. The demands of his job, easily handled for the first year and a half, now sapped his energy terribly. He was grateful the force was now using automobiles. They saved him time and energy. He could always pull off the road and rest a bit. And the heat was debilitating. He hadn't got used to it yet; maybe he never would. He often sat in the lobby of the Blaine Lake Hotel, where it was cool, just sat there, taking one careful breath after another. He could have lain down right there on the lobby floor and let people walk around him.

One day in the summer of 1917, as he was forcing himself to go out in the burning street, he saw John Patterson striding purposefully into the lobby. They met near the registration desk, where the proprietor, Alex Armstrong, was leaning on the counter reading a newspaper.

"Hello, John. Hot enough for you?" Sometimes Wilson was surprised to hear himself talking like a person from the prairies.

"Jack, I need to talk to you, if you have a minute," Patterson said. He looked serious.

"Oh? What about?"

John Patterson took Wilson's arm and moved a few steps away from the front desk. He lowered his voice.

"It's about Jessie, you seeing Jessie, I mean. I want you to tell me . . . Well, you know there are rumours going around that you're a married man, and I have to ask you if they're true."

"No, they're not true. I *was* married, but my wife died after I left the old country."

"Oh? Well, I'm sorry to hear that."

"It's all right. It's almost three years ago. But you know how stories get twisted."

"Oh, sure, I know what it's like in a small place. Did you have any children?"

"No, we didn't, and I'm glad about that now. Under the circumstances."

John Patterson clapped Wilson on his thin shoulder. "Sorry to bring it up, Jack, but I had to ask—because of Jessie, you understand. She's got so fond of you."

"That's all right. But I'd better move along. I've got to check out a lead up north."

"Come for supper if you're back in time. You need to put on a few pounds."

"Thanks. I will."

After the door closed behind John Patterson, Wilson walked to the desk. Alex Armstrong put down the paper he'd been pretending to read.

"I was just telling John there that my wife passed away after I left the old country."

"Yes, I couldn't help hearing. That's too bad. What happened, if you don't mind my asking?"

"Well, it's quite a story." Jack's expression implied that there was something scandalous about his wife's death. "Yes, sir, it's quite a story. I'll have to tell you sometime." He waved as he stepped out onto the street. The heat took his breath away: heat like a powerful presence, rippling over his skin. He hoped it would bring on a storm. Rain would feel so good.

∽

In spite of how ill he'd felt for so long, Jack Wilson wasn't prepared for the shock in store when he saw the doctor at the end of the summer. He sat on the examining table, bare to the waist, as the doctor's cold stethoscope explored his thin back and chest, raising goose pimples on his white skin.

"Another deep breath in."

He inhaled shallowly, unsteadily, his breath making a strange clicking and gurgling sound in the quiet office.

"Now out."

It took a long time to breathe out, as if there was something in the way. The doctor's expression changed.

"Deeper now."

"I can't. I haven't been able to for ages." He exhaled, another shallow, prolonged breath.

The doctor listened. Frowned. Took his temperature. Probed some more. Tapped Wilson's chest above the clavicle, a dull, thudding sound. Peered in his throat. Then folded the stethoscope and handed Wilson his shirt.

Jack's hands trembled as he fumbled buttons into buttonholes. He didn't give a damn any more what happened to him. He just wanted to lie down on this table and never get up.

"I'm sorry to have to tell you, Jack, but you have TB."

"Oh, no." His head and shoulders slumped, his worst fears confirmed. "You're sure?"

"Yes. Ninety-nine per cent positive it's tuberculosis."

Tuberculosis. A dreaded word. Tantamount to a death sentence in 1917, almost thirty years before the discovery of the antibiotic streptomycin. He knew how deadly it was. Only ten per cent survived.

"And it sounds pretty advanced. It's not like small pox or typhoid, you know. You can have it a long time before you feel ill. Do you have anyone to look after you?"

"No, I don't. Are you saying I won't be able to work?"

The doctor shook his head. "You'll soon be so ill you'll have to be in bed. You should be there now."

"Can you give me anything?" Jack asked, without much hope.

"No. Nothing. With care—good food, complete bed rest—you might get better. Without it . . ." He shrugged and gestured, palms up.

Outside, on the street, Wilson shivered, though the day was warm. What was he going to do? He wished, not for the first time, that he'd never left the old country. Well, the first thing he had to do was report to headquarters.

When he informed his superior of his illness, he was discharged from the RNWMP and asked to turn in his uniform. He was supplied with a tent and instructed to quarantine himself.

Jack Wilson was a very sick man, far from home and family, with little money, no clothes but hand-me-downs, and no place to go, since the first sanatorium in the province would not open till October. The sight of that lonely tent on the edge of town as cool fall evenings drew in would have stirred pity in the hardest of hearts.

Jessie Patterson did not have a hard heart, nor, it seems, did her parents. They did everything they could to help Wilson. He came to their house every day and sat shivering in a chair while Jessie and her mother applied poultices to his thin chest and back. Later, when it became obvious he was too sick to be in a tent with winter coming, they nursed him through the worst of it, a brave (or foolhardy) thing to do in more ways than one. Morally courageous, since the wagging tongues were sure to wag faster, and physically and emotionally courageous, given the wildly contagious nature of the disease.

And so Wilson lived through the long winter of 1917–1918, looked after primarily by Jessie, who, he said, was the soul of goodness. "She was good to me above everyone else," he would often say later. He was determined, if he recovered, to spend a lifetime repaying Jessie for her kindness.

At some point that winter, he asked Jessie to marry him. He explained, however, that his wife was not dead, but that he was divorcing her because she was a woman with no morals whatsoever who had tricked him into marrying her. The divorce would soon be final. Now Jessie understood why Jack sometimes looked so sad.

And, yes, she would marry him.

∼

Many young women Jessie's age would have had second thoughts about commitment to the romantic mounted policeman when he was no longer romantic or a policeman and lay coughing up bits of his lungs in a bed she'd probably given up for him.

But tuberculosis still had about it an aura of refinement; it was seen as an artist's disease, singling out those with delicate, aesthetic natures. The Latin root of *consumption*, the nineteenth-century word for the disease, reinforced that idea: *con* meaning "completely," plus *sumere*, "to take up from under," an etymology that suggests the body is being taken up to some loftier plane.

Nineteenth- and early twentieth-century literature supported the mythology, and even doctors subscribed to its theory. When Robert Koch discovered the tubercle bacillus in 1882, the public, and many in the medical profession, were skeptical. They were reluctant to give up the belief that the disease was caused chiefly by the victim's own delicate constitution.

Tuberculosis was thus regarded as a genteel disease leading to an easy death. The transcendental beauty of fictional heroes and heroines was no doubt based on the sparkling eyes and flush of low-grade fever. The more disgusting manifestations of this illness of fluids—sweat, sputum, blood—were conveniently omitted from novels, plays and the opera.

And, of course, the gentle death of nineteenth-century fiction was just that: fiction. Hemorrhaging to death, as many did, was terrifying.

There were only two known treatments of tuberculosis at the time. One was complete bed rest with plenty of fresh air. The other being tried in the east was artificial pneumothorax, in which the affected lung was collapsed by air injected between it and the chest wall. Since the bacilli needed air to thrive, the theory was that healing would take place as the lung "rested." The air dissipated into the body in two or three weeks, with much attendant discomfort, and the whole procedure was repeated.

∾

Slowly over that long, quiet winter, John Wilson began to recover. As spring approached, strength seeped back into his wasted body; the fever subsided, and he began to gain weight. By early spring, he was up and around, gaining strength every day.

He must have had a little money put aside, or borrowed some, as he moved to the Blaine Lake Hotel in the spring. He spent a lot of time just sitting in the lobby and going for walks—a little farther every time—and visiting Jessie. His tangled domestic affairs seemed secondary for the moment. Jack Wilson was surprised and grateful to be alive.

In April, the snow melted, the ditches ran, and the sun brought comfort to body and soul. Rude, noisy, dirty—a typical prairie spring. A gentler spring had arrived long ago across the sea. It was the sixth spring Jack had missed, but he was not homesick. Home was wherever Jessie was.

Chapter x

∾ FIRST FOOTING ∾

December 31, 1917. Another Hogmanay. And tomorrow their tenth wedding anniversary. The sixth Hogmanay Jack has missed. The fifth anniversary.

Her parents' house gleamed. Every speck of dust banished, every smooth surface polished to death. Polly had done the same in her own house back in Kilncadzow before she came. Every cupboard scrubbed out, every curtain washed, every floor and window shining, not a thing left unwashed, unironed, or unpolished. Not a thing out of place. How you left your house when the clock struck twelve on First Footing night is how it would be all year. It was bad luck to forget anything. But she needed to be here with her family this night, needed to tell them of her decision, and to ask their assistance and their blessing.

Her father wandered into the parlour.

"Aye, Polly, have you seen my slippers anywhere?" He was all dressed up, the shine on his black shoes deafening.

"No, Father, I haven't. Mother's probably put them in your cupboard."

"Washed them, starched them and ironed them more like." He grinned at her.

Polly laughed and William Hutchison patted her shoulder. He loved all his children, but Polly had a special place in his heart. She always was such a cheery little person, and she'd been such a brave lass these past years.

"And where are the bairns?"

"George finally agreed to take a nap. He made me promise to get him up for First Footing. And Ella keeled over an hour ago."

"Worn out with all the blethering, poor bairns, I don't wonder." But her father looked with satisfaction around the room. The small fire had been laid in the grate. It would be lit and die down, then a new one would be laid before midnight. The unopened bottle of whiskey sat on the sideboard, ready for next year's dram. Consciences had all been examined, none more diligently than William Hutchison's, for the good suffer more from conscience than any. Old slights all forgiven. He rubbed his hands in anticipation.

Helen Hutchison bustled in. She had changed into her good blue dress, the first time she'd been seen without an apron for days.

"D'you think you should you light the fire, Father? Lizzie and Archie will be here any minute. Jim and Nellie and the others, too."

"If you tell me what you've done wi' my slippers, I'll light the fire."
Helen laughed and patted his smooth cheek. "Happy Hogmanay,
Father. You're looking that handsome I hardly know ye."

"Now is that a compliment or is it not? It's hard to tell, isn't it?" He
winked at Polly, as calls of "Happy Hogmanay" heralded the arrival
of Jim and family, with Lizzie and Archie close behind.

When they were all assembled and had exchanged news, Polly
knew the moment had come.

"I must talk to you all while the bairns are sleeping. You know I've
had no word from Jack since last June."

"Still nothing?" Jim asked. "I was hoping he'd have remembered
your anniversary." It was only for her present happiness he wished it.
He had concluded she'd be better off in the long run if she never
heard from the scoundrel again.

"No. Nothing. But I've made a decision and I'm hoping you'll all
stand behind me for I need your help."

She had their undivided attention. Lizzie moved across the room to
sit beside Polly and take her hand. Nellie glanced at her parents.

"I must go to Canada and look for Jack."

There was a moment's shocked silence.

"But, Polly, you don't even know where he is or if he's—" William
began. A look from his wife silenced him.

"It's all right, Mother. Father's right. I don't know if Jack's alive. But
I feel so afraid for him. He sounded so ill the last time he wrote. And
who does he have to take care of him in that big, lonely country?"

"When are you thinking of going, Polly?" This from Lizzie.

"In April. It will be spring there by then. I've been putting by some
money and have almost enough for the fare."

"I think you should wait until the war is over," her father said.

"Aye," Jim agreed. "Who knows what could happen with German
submarines still out there? Think of the *Lusitania*." The fire crackled
in the sudden silence.

"And that terrible explosion in Halifax last month, right where
you'd be landing," Nellie added.

"Six and a half years is long enough to wait." Polly's voice wavered
for a moment. Then she straightened up, and her voice recovered.

"Even if Jack is dead, I must know, don't you see? I have to find out for the children's sake as well as my own."

"Yes," said her mother. "Polly has got to go on with her life, with or without Jack, we must understand that. We'll take the children—won't we, Father?—till you get back. It probably wouldn't be for too long."

"But what if it's TB John's got?" Elizabeth said. "With his lungs it probably is, and you know how contagious that is. At least the children have a mother now."

"Now, Lizzie," William said. "If Polly's made up her mind, there's no use making it worse. It's hard enough for her." And for me, he wanted to say. To see my sweet daughter go off God knows where to God knows what. But you mustn't impose your will on your children when they are no longer children. "Yes, of course we'll take the bairns. It will be good for us, eh, Mother? Make us young again."

"Just try to think what you would do if it was Archie," Polly said, and Elizabeth gave her a sudden fierce hug.

"You never know," said her mother. "Jack could be home by then. Or at least you might know when he's coming."

Jim got up and went outside to have a smoke. In his mother's house, even that was not allowed today. Not until First Footing. Who will it be? he wondered, the first man across the threshold. Probably David Thomson. He lit up, blowing the smoke out into the damp, foggy night. Polly shouldn't go, he felt it in his bones. There was just more heartbreak in store for her over there. But maybe that's what it would take for her to face the truth. Jack Wilson did not want to come home. That should be obvious to anybody.

Inside, William Hutchison raked the ashes from the fire and scooped them into the copper scuttle. Helen swept the hearth clean as he carried out the ashes in preparation for the new year, the ritual they had performed together each year for forty-five years. The clock on the mantel pointed a quarter to the hour.

Upstairs, Polly roused a sleepy George to take part in the festivities. She felt such enormous relief. This coming year would settle things one way or the other.

By the time the clock began to strike midnight and the town church bells pealed out, they were all back in the warm room.

"Let's open the window, Mother," William said, "and let the old year out." They pushed the casement window wide. "There it goes," William said, and everyone laughed.

"Yes. And now we wait for the First Foot," said William. "I wonder who it will be?" His children smiled at each other. They knew how he loved this ceremony, and they knew he knew very well who the First Foot would be since he would have arranged it, as always, with a dark-haired man. A blond man was unlucky because he might once have been a Norse invader. This varied depending on where you lived in Scotland, but here the First Foot had to be dark, or bad luck would befall the house. In a small village like the "Slam" this kept the dark-haired men busy.

At the sound of the last chime the whiskey bottle was opened with great ceremony, and small crystal glasses passed around.

"Just a wee bit of insurance," said William.

George stared wide-eyed at the door, for the First Foot is rather like Santa Claus.

"To 1918," his grandfather said. "To a healthy and prosperous year for everyone, and a happy new year to us all." The grownups clinked glasses. "And to a safe and successful journey for our Polly," William said.

Grateful tears filled Polly's eyes as her family drank to that. Then Helen, Polly and Lizzie went to the kitchen for trays of sandwiches and shortbread. The traditional and delicious black bun would be brought in by the First Foot.

At the hammering on the door, George shrieked. With a great flourish, William swung the door wide.

"Happy Hogmanay to the Hutchisons!" cried the red-haired man lurching across the threshold. He had obviously started on his not-so-wee dram long before midnight. Fog rolled in the open door behind him.

"Oh, dear! It's Clyde Barrow." Mary Hutchison tried not to sound upset. "Where's David?"

"Here!" called a voice, and the dark-haired David Thomson stepped in with a bottle in one hand and a beautifully wrapped parcel in the other: the black bun full of walnuts and cinnamon to be shared with a wee dram and some shortbread. He handed the bottle to William and the black bun to Helen. "Happy new year to the Hutchisons."

"Ooops. Sorry, friends." Clyde Barrow's good-natured face fell. "I'll go out and come in again," he said. And he did.

But it wasn't the same. It wasn't the same at all.

Chapter XI

∽ HE WAS A GOOD BOY ∾

Having lied to Jessie about his wife, Jack Wilson encouraged her to write to his sister Mary. Wilson offered to mail the letter, and in due course brought Jessie this reply:

> Royal Infirmary,
> Glasgow.
> 4th March, 1918.

My dear sister Jessie,

I have just had your letter read to me by Mr. Haxwell and he has a short-hand clerk taking this down. Oh, Jessie, I am dying and the doctors say the end will be here in about one hour. If I could only have lived until I seen you and John I would have died content. I am not afraid to die and since I know that John is going to have you to look after him it makes it easier. Jessie, I feel as I had known you a long time and I am going to tell you something about John if my strength only holds out.

He was a good boy and was my mother's favourite child and she died with her head on his arm. After that he tried to follow her footsteps and was good to the poor people, he never drank or smoked. He joined the Highlanders and made a splendid-looking soldier. I used to be proud to walk down the street with him as people would turn around and look at him. He had lots of money and made friends with all the boys in his regiment. He got the gold medal two years in succession for being the smartest soldier in the brigade. Ask him to give you a look at his medals if he has not already done so. They are lovely. Then the change came,

Jessie, and my heart was sore for him. One Glasgow holiday he hired a pleasure steamer and took all the boys in his company on a pleasure trip to Rothesay, he also took all the girls from a dressmaking shop on the trip and that was where he met the woman who ruined him.

A few weeks later he told me he was getting married. He had hardly known the girl a month, and I did not like her but I could not get him to stop the marriage but I got him to put it off for about nine months, that was until New Year's Day. I was sure she was only after his money.

She went home then and I think John only seen her twice during the nine months. He spoke to me once during that time about it and said he had asked her to break off the engagement but she would not do it and threatened him with an action in the Court for Breach of Promise if she was left. John was afraid of the disgrace and went through with the marriage. She made great preparations at his expense. It must have cost him several thousand dollars. They were married on New Year's Day and went to London the same day. They were only gone 4 days and he returned very unhappy-looking and about two months after that I knew John was not sleeping in the house but he tried to hide from everyone that he was not getting along with her and that he was leading a miserable life.

About ten months after that a boy was born and I told John that they would get along better after that as the boy would draw them together, but if you had only seen his face when he said that they get along worse as he was not his boy. He said they had never had any husband and wife connections and they had never slept in the same room since they were married. Oh, Jessie, it was awful to see him suffering when people were congratulating him on getting a son. John had always been a great boy for dances but after that he stopped going to them altogether and mixed up with no one. One night about 5 or 6 weeks later John went home for some papers about 10 P.M. he found a man in bed with her. He picked him up and took him out in the street where everyone could see, and John thrashed him until I thought he was going to kill him. Next morning John left for Holland. Dear Jessie, John tried every way to get along with her but it was no use. She was bad out and out.

He has had a hard life, Jessie, but you are his first love and I know he will make you happy, he must love you very dear or he would not give up all his property for you. He is upright and honourable and you can trust your life to him.

Now, Jessie, I am getting weak and I want to write to John yet. I can die happier now knowing he is in your care. It is lonesome to die here alone but I am not afraid as I have always tried to be a good girl and with my dying breath I pray to the Lord that John and you will be happy.

Try to cheer him up, Jessie, as when he hears of my death he will feel it bad. Good-bye, sister Jessie, and may the blessing of a dying girl rest on you always.

Your dying sister,
Mary

The following letter accompanied the previous one:

Royal Infirmary,
Glasgow.
4-3-18.

Dear Jessie,

Having heard that Mary was dying here I hurried to see her. She was able to speak for about two hours before the end came. I read your letter to her and she had me get a shorthand writer to take down the enclosed reply. Miss Jessie, it was the most pathetic deathbed I ever was at in all my long experience. I married the father and mother and christened all the children and now they are all dead but John. Mary was a good girl and she was not afraid to die; the end came very peacefully and the last words she said were "Father, Mother, Isa, Sandy, I am coming. Good-bye, Jessie and John." Then a smile came over her face and she passed away. I could not keep the tears away and I noticed the two doctors and two nurses were crying also. I buried her beside her father and mother where John has a monument worthy of them.

His father and mother were respected by everyone. His mother was always working among the poor people and helping them along with money and food.

John was her favourite boy but he has led a very unhappy life since she died. I do not usually approve of divorce but in this case I advised John to get one long ago. It is a very sad story and Mary did not have time to tell you half of what the poor boy suffered. I am an old man of 76 years of age and I never had a case where a boy suffered more than he had done.

In conclusion I ask you to be worthy of him and try and make the balance of his life happy, I can trust him to be good and true to you, and I only hope that I will live long enough to meet you both. Meanwhile accept my prayers for your future happiness and may the blessing of the Almighty God be with you both, now and forever.

Your sincere friend,
F. M. Haxwell

P.S. I am unable to write now and have to get a typist so please excuse this.

The upright and honourable John Wilson wrote both these letters himself.

Jessie apparently found nothing odd about the letters. She carefully saved them in a large brown envelope, along with the many letters from Jack, letters he had written when he was away on police business and when she had gone away herself in February 1917. At that time she may have been trying to break off with him, as Jack wrote a strange letter, telling her he would pick her up and register her as an alien so she couldn't leave Blaine Lake. That letter was signed "Lindsay," Wilson's second name.

Jack Wilson was well liked by many in Blaine Lake, and that spring of 1918 they saw a man very much down on his luck. As he gained strength day by day, the town of Blaine Lake offered him the job of notary public and justice of the peace. It would pay him a little and not tax his strength too much. He had discharged his duties as a Mountie admirably, and in spite of the rumours about his marital status, the townspeople respected that. He kept his own counsel and could be trusted with people's private affairs. He was also hired to sell cars for Larson Brothers Auto Dealers, and things began to look brighter. He would bide his time till he could get back into the Mounties.

◠◡

Meanwhile, in Kilncadzow, a worried Elizabeth helped her sister pack. Usually when people went travelling, it was for a holiday at the seaside, to take a pleasure boat on the River Clyde, or to spend a few days in Glasgow to shop and go to the music hall. Happy occasions. It was difficult for Elizabeth to know what kind of face to put on this journey of Polly's. It was anything but a holiday, more like a quest, if one had to put a name to it. To pretend they were happy about her going would have been a lie, and yet Polly needed their blessings.

The faint hope that word from Jack would change her course remained just that. January had dragged on, wet and gloomy, February not much better, and Polly quietly began to get ready. She sewed late into the night, after her other work was done: a new tweed suit, a spring dress, an extra skirt. Her mother came one day with a dainty lace-trimmed camisole and nightgown, and Polly was grateful for the implication in this generous gesture. She could almost believe that she was just going to a reunion with a husband who loved her.

March came and went with still no word, and Polly asked Jim to book a ticket for an early April sailing. Money was raised among the family so she could sail on the *Mauretania*, a luxury liner that wasn't likely to be mistaken for a troop ship by German submarines. Other relatives and friends gave Polly gifts of money for her journey.

Polly packed her suitcase—a large, light-brown patent leather case with leather and brass fittings, a gift from Elizabeth and Archie. And, of course, a trunk, since there was no way of knowing how long she'd be away. Warm sweaters for the deck of a ship in April and a prairie spring; extra skirts and blouses, stockings, underthings; her Bible, the one they'd presented to her when she was Slamannan Sunday school scholar. And, most important, a photograph of her and the children, taken about a year after Jack left, all of them looking a wee bit lost and solemn. She needed their faces to look at till she could hold them again.

And so, in her new suit with the pin John bought her on their Dublin honeymoon fastened to the lapel, Polly Wilson bade good-bye to her family and her children and set off for Canada.

Chapter XII
ᘳ THE QUEST ᘰ

The *Mauretania*, Cunard's golden ship, would become an Atlantic legend. Indeed, by the time Polly walked aboard, the liner was already famous. In "The Song of the Machines," by Rudyard Kipling, she is described as a "monstrous nine-decked city" and standing alongside her, the metaphor seemed apt. Kipling even managed—well, tried— to wax lyrical about her "thirty thousand horses and some screws," which tells a lot about how the *Mauretania* affected people. She was a sister ship to the ill-fated *Lusitania*. Both ships were launched in 1907, in the last decade before the war, when emigration accounted for a huge volume of business for steamship companies.

"The North Atlantic is no place to be in April," said the man who crossed in 1912. Even on the huge ships many got seasick, and in 1918 there were German submarines to think about on the dark nights. Polly had a second-cabin ticket, which supplied a modest but attractively furnished cabin with a bunk rather than the brass bed provided in first class, and she shared a communal bathroom and lavatories down the passageway. Second-cabin passengers had their own decks, sheltered and open; their own dining saloons and smoking rooms, their own libraries, gymnasia, purser's office, and writing rooms.

Polly spent many hours writing letters to be mailed in Halifax. She'd had lots of practice in the epistolary art in the years since Jack left. She could not get over the size of the ship. The *Mauretania*'s four smokestacks were each wide enough for two cars to drive through abreast with plenty of room to spare, and were sixty-five feet high (the height of a prairie grain elevator). The ship's statistics were printed on folders that Polly sent home to Jim, Archie and the Joiner. They would be interested to know that steel plates more than an inch thick formed the skin, or shell plating, of the ship. Some were fifty feet long and weighed five tons, and it had taken four million rivets to assemble the hull and superstructure. "Isn't that rivetting?" she wrote to Jim. Somehow, being away from home, and doing something about her situation, had lightened her heart.

Polly's travelling companions included many young women going to Canada to join husbands they'd met and married during the war. They were just girls, really, most of them younger than Polly by at least ten years. Their journeys would take them to lonely sod shacks on the prairies, one-roomed cabins in northern bush country, and towns and cities along the route. Whenever she was asked, Polly said she was going to meet her husband, a mounted policeman, and that is what is written on the passenger list as her reason for travelling. Polly was sea-sick, and would have agreed with Dr. Johnson, who said that going to sea was like going to prison with the chance of being drowned.

Finally, the ship was escorted into Halifax harbour, where the worst disaster in Canadian history had occurred just four months earlier. A French munitions ship carrying almost two thousand tons of explosives collided with a Belgian relief ship in the narrows. The explosion killed eighteen thousand people and seriously injured four thousand more. What she could see of the city looked like a war zone.

The *Mauretania* docked at Halifax harbour at 11:28 A.M., April 12, 1918. The medical examination was short. The examiners were most interested in anyone showing signs of the dreaded eye disease trachoma. From there Polly passed through customs and on to the CPR train that would take her west.

From the train she looked out at the same landscape John had six years earlier. She talked with other women from the boat and watched as they pressed their faces to the window, trembling with anticipation of the first sight of a beloved face. She saw them greeted at small and large station platforms, engulfed in passionate embraces. She waved at them from the window as the train moved on. And on. And on. No wonder people could come here and never be heard from again. It was just too big.

As they drew closer to Regina, Polly gathered her things together. She would stop there and make inquiries.

"Will we get to see that handsome Mountie of yours?" asked an Irish woman who had seen the pictures Polly carried.

"Oh, I'm afraid not. He doesn't know when to expect me."

"Ah well, it's soon you'll be seeing him. That's the main thing."

But, Polly thought, wouldn't it be grand to see him standing there? And finally, on April 18, Regina: clusters of buildings on a flat, muddy plain, with patches of dirty snow on their lee sides. In the bright sunlight there was a raw newness about many of them. Other, jerrybuilt places already showed the signs of wear she had noticed all along the train route. She had lived all her life in a place where houses were built to withstand the centuries. But the well-developed city centre surprised her, with its tall brick buildings, handsome churches and lovely big houses.

Trainmen blew whistles and signalled importantly as the train, with screeching brakes and clouds of steam, slowed to a stop. The station platform teemed with people, some waving joyfully at familiar faces, others clutching tickets and valises. Large baggage carts rumbled through the crowd. There was such energy in this country, such an air of excitement. Her heart leapt at the sight of a uniformed Mountie on the platform. Of course, it wasn't Jack but it suddenly made him seem much closer. Polly's arms felt strangely weak and they shook as she took down her suitcase. She said her good-byes to the women going farther west and finally stepped off the train, grateful for the conductor's firm hand on her arm.

She stood on the platform for a few moments, trying to calm herself, then picked up her valise and walked towards the station. When she found a telephone, her heart pounded and she had to force herself to crank the handle before she lost her nerve. Her voice shook as she asked the operator for the Mounted Police headquarters.

"Royal North West Mounted Police. Constable Brickton speaking."

"Hello. I am trying to locate Corporal John Wilson."

"I'm sorry I don't know Corporal Wilson's whereabouts. Just hold on please, ma'am, and I'll try to find out for you."

Polly waited, gripping the phone as if her life depended on it, as if it would hold her up if the news was bad. Then the constable was back.

"We think if you phone the Prince Albert detachment, they might be able to tell you his whereabouts." He gave her the number and wished her well.

With a deep breath, she cranked the phone again.

Chapter XIII

∾ IS IT REALLY YOU? ∾

Early in 1918, the Royal North West Mounted Police called for five hundred volunteers for an overseas cavalry unit, and on April 18, Jack Wilson drove to Prince Albert to volunteer. Earlier in the war, Commissioner A. Bowen Perry had offered a squadron, but Prime Minister Robert Borden said no; the Mounted Police were needed in western Canada. With the creation of provincial policing in 1917, Borden gave the okay for an RNWMP cavalry squadron.

To Wilson, the call for volunteers presented an opportunity to serve his country, and to straighten out his personal life. While overseas, he could decide what to do about Jessie. But it was not to be. The call for five hundred men was answered by more than seven hundred, so the force was not constrained to choose any but the most fit, the most eligible, and a bout with TB was not the best preparation for cavalry service.

"I'm sorry, Jack. We have far more men than we need," Superintendent Walton Routledge told him.

"If you're worried about my health, I'm feeling very well now. And the doctor's given me a clean bill of health."

"That's good news."

"Yes, sir. When do you think I might get back on general duty?"

"Give it a few more months. You want to make sure you're one hundred per cent before you reapply."

The phone on the superintendent's desk rang. "Royal North West Mounted Police. Superintendent Routledge speaking."

Wilson stood looking out the window, waiting for the conversation to end.

"Yes. Just a moment, please. He's right here." Routledge handed the phone to a surprised Wilson.

"Hello. John Wilson speaking."

"Jack? Oh, Jack, is it really you?"

Wilson's knees almost buckled at the familiar Scottish voice in his ear.

"Polly? Is that you? Where are you?"

"You'll never believe it, Jack. I'm in Regina. Your office here put me on to Prince Albert. Are you all right? I've been so worried!"

"Yes, no, well, oh, Lord, what a surprise!" He felt the blood leave his face, and everything outside the window looked strangely far away. He gripped the edge of Routledge's desk for support. The superintendent looked at him with concern.

"I've been very sick with TB. I almost died. That's why I haven't written."

"Oh, I *knew* something was wrong. That's what I told them at home."

"I'm getting better now. I can't believe this. I was just in the office trying to get back overseas."

"You haven't joined up?" Polly's said, her voice fearful.

"No. They have more than they need for now. Where are you phoning from?"

"I'm still at the station. Oh, Jack, should I catch the next train to Prince Albert?"

"No! No, don't do that. Take the train to Saskatoon tomorrow and I'll meet you there midafternoon sometime."

"Aye, I will. Where should I meet you?"

"Just stay at the station. Then we'll decide what to do."

"I'll be there. I can't believe I'm really talking to you. I doubt I'll sleep a wink tonight."

"It will be good to see you, too." He tried to sound pleased. What else could he do?

Chapter XIV

⟶ A PRAIRIE TRIANGLE ⟵

As Jack Wilson drove to meet his wife the next day, his mind was working overtime. After the initial shock of the phone call, all the ramifications of the lie he'd been living leapt to his mind.

If he told Polly he'd fallen in love with another woman and sent her back home, the scandal he'd left behind would pale by comparison. He hated the thought of it. Polly had told him people were impressed with his being a Mountie. And those Blaine Lake people who whispered about him being married, wouldn't they just love it? He couldn't wait to get out of that place. He hated it now.

But that wasn't the worst of it. The worst of it was Jessie, who'd been so faithful and true through everything—his TB, the rumours—and who expected to marry him soon. He couldn't bear the thought of her finding out he still had a wife. And, worse yet, his wife was *here*.

He'd have to take her somewhere far away from Blaine Lake while he thought out what to do. Just the thought of Jessie finding out made him want to cry. He'd told her last night he was going to Regina to look for a job that paid enough for them to get married.

The trip to Saskatoon was interminable. It was cold driving, and the hints of green here and there as he drove depressed him even more. It wasn't fair. He'd been ill for so long and was just starting to feel hopeful again; it was finally spring, and now this.

∿

On the station platform, Polly walked back and forth, glancing often at the road where Jack would come; she couldn't sit still for fear of missing the first sight of him. Another train arrived, with people stepping off, looking as disoriented as she'd felt yesterday in Regina. Two Mounties got off the train, joking with the conductor. She couldn't help it, every time she saw that uniform, her heart seemed to turn over.

She walked around a pile of trunks, suitcases, carpetbags and boxes tied with sturdy rope, foreign names printed carefully on their tops and sides. She smiled as newcomers were met by families and burst into excited talk she couldn't understand. She liked the sound of their laughter, their fierce embraces.

She wore the suit she'd travelled in—the other skirts were hopelessly creased—but everything else was fresh. She'd washed her hair in the hotel in Regina last night and had a real bath. And hadn't that felt good after the long trip and the spit baths in the tiny train compartment? She'd scarcely slept, since she had to be up at six to catch the train, but she didn't feel tired. Her hair felt different, full of electricity in the dry air. She felt that way herself.

And suddenly there he was. Not in uniform as she'd imagined him, but in a tweed suit that hung from his shoulders, and pale and thin enough to break her heart. Then his arms were around her.

"Thank God, I've got my own at last," Jack said.

The wait was finally over. In her excitement at seeing her husband, Polly didn't notice his nervousness or the dismay he tried to conceal.

The plan he had formulated on the way to Saskatoon was to take Polly to Regina and look for work there. That would give him time to think of what to do. It was a long drive to Regina, but he had worked in Saskatoon, knew people there, and nothing must get back to Blaine Lake, just forty miles away. And the diversion of driving would cover his nervousness.

"Back to Regina? Oh, Jack, do we have to go today?"

"I know, Polly, but I figured it out on the way here. I need to find work, and there's nothing here." He was already loading her suitcase and trunk in the back of the car.

"Oh, well, whatever you think is best. I don't mind, as long as we're together."

"Yes," Jack said. "You can give me all the news from home on the drive." And so they set off for Regina, a nine-hour drive at twenty miles an hour.

Polly did most of the talking, telling him all about George and Ella, the things they said now and did, and news of her family and his, their friends and neighbours, and which boys would never come home from the war. And how some would never be the same.

"Poor William Angus. You should have seen him when he got the Victoria Cross, he looked so confused at all the commotion."

Polly talked and talked and talked, as if everything she'd wanted to tell him for six long years was right there on the tip of her tongue, just waiting for him to appear.

"Are you sure we shouldn't go back home? I miss everyone already, and I hate to leave the children too long."

"No. I want to wait and see. If I get back in the force, we can send for them. I'd rather do police work than anything."

Well, she thought, he was her husband. It was his decision to make, and she must go along with it. And after making all the decisions for years now, it was a relief.

It was chilly driving, with some snow still caught in the stubble of last year's crops, but exhiliarating, too. She marvelled at the space, the impossibly large sky, more amazing now than from the train. She was interested in everything: the farms and villages they passed through, the sight of coyotes, and deer, and once a V of beautiful white geese flying low, their undersides tinged pink from the setting sun. And when the sun set behind them in a spectacular array of fiery reds, golds and oranges, with streams of light beaming down between gold-rimmed clouds, like a picture straight out of the Old Testament, she said she had never seen anything so beautiful.

Jack looked tired and strained. Several times on the drive he reached down to pull a bottle out from under the seat and down a few swallows. He always had liked his wee dram, but not like that, straight from the bottle, and as if he really needed it. Well, he was tired, and maybe he did need it.

In Regina, the Wilsons rented a room in a boarding house at 2039 Rose Street, run by a Mrs. Eileen Wismer, a motherly soul who took to Polly immediately. The two-storey brick house with a front veranda was almost indistinguishable from the neighbours on either side. Here the couple would stay for five and a half months—at least Polly would; Jack was often gone for days at a time.

Their marital relations resumed immediately. Terrible of him, "taking advantage" of her like that, some would say—and did say later. But given the mores of the time, it had likely been a very long time since he'd made love to a woman; and also, not to do so would have made Polly suspicious. He needed time. And perhaps he realized what a cruelty it would be to reject her at the end of her long journey. Polly wrote a joyful letter home to tell them she had arrived safely and all was well.

Within days of her arrival, Polly Wilson was pregnant.

Wilson applied for a position with the Canadian Military Police Corps, CMPC, a federal police force that dealt with enforcing the Military Service Act, MSA, or conscription. Because of his experience in the Mounties, he was hired immediately, and he gave up his jobs in Blaine Lake.

The flow of letters from Jack Wilson's pen were now directed to Jessie, his "darling wee girl" in Blaine Lake. He would say later that he tried at this time to give up Jessie. His actions say otherwise. Jessie had been his almost constant companion since the past summer, and the powerful bond they'd forged when he was ill was stronger than any sense of moral obligation.

When one loves like this, the temptation to say the beloved's name is always there, and John told Polly about Jessie, how good she was to him when he was ill. No doubt he portrayed her as just a friend, the daughter of his good friends the Pattersons. But his expression as he spoke of her, his need to say her name, was not lost on Polly.

Wilson lay awake nights beside his wife, fighting with himself. And losing, again and again. He should give up Jessie, for her sake, but he couldn't bear the thought. Every chance he got, under any pretext, he went to see her, and between times, the love letters continued unabated.

> Department of Justice,
> Military Service Branch
> Dominion Police
> Tuesday Night, 18th June, 1918
> 6:45 P.M.

My Dearest Wee Girl,

I got your letter yesterday morning and how sad it made me I cannot tell you, Jessie. Oh, Dearest, I know it is lonesome for you at Blaine Lake and how I wish I could take you away now, Jessie, and make you happy, but, Dearest, I want to be strong again before I take you away. I would not wait a minute if I was only sure I was all clear in my lungs. Dearest, if you only knew how miserable it is for me here alone. I have not chummed up with anyone and every night when I go to the tent I wonder if there is any other person in this world with as few friends as I have.

Jessie, I would gladly give my life anytime if it would help you any. You are all I have in this world to care for and I love you with all my heart. You have been the kindest friend I have known since Mother died, and although I never bothered much about religion I often pray now that I get well again and strong and get a chance to repay you for all you have done for me. That is from the bottom of my heart, Dearest, and there are tears in my eyes when I am writing this. I am yours to do as you want, Jessie Dearest, and when we are married it will be like a new life to me and what a pleasure it will be to love and to care for you and never to be parted till Death comes.

Jessie, I am so lonely and sad tonight . . . When I think of you being so unhappy at Blaine Lake it makes me so sad and downhearted, and, Jessie, I have tried to get away so much this last week but we are so busy with work it is not possible to start on the Dukobors yet. I don't think I will get up before the 1st, Dearest. I will try hard to get away before that but all the responsibility of the work is on my shoulders and everyone seems to rely on me to help them but the men are getting more experienced every day and that makes it easier.

He then goes on to arrange to meet Jessie in Prince Albert and take her on a four-day holiday at her cousin's farm near Kinistino.

. . . and it would be far better out at the farm where we could go for walks anywhere. I don't like Blaine Lake except for you, and at Mrs. Dunlop's we would have every minute to ourselves and I don't think she would say a word if we sat up late . . . And, Jessie, I will try to make you happy and I will kiss you this time whether you slap me or not . . .

The Boss is back just now, Jessie, and he got word from Ottawa this morning that in our Province we have the smallest number of Deserters who have not been arrested and he is as proud as a peacock over it and says, "Wilson, you are a wonder." We have only 299 deserters at large. Of course there are hundreds more who have never reported at all . . . But it is hard work, Dearest, some nights I am too tired to sleep, all day long it is just a continual rush of telegrams and long distance calls . . .

Now, Dearest, I am going to stop and go and post your letter then home and the tent. Oh, Jessie, it is lonesome. I am sitting here every night looking out the window all alone and on Sundays it is just the same. Dearest, if love and kindness will make you happy when we are married you will be the happiest wee girl in the world. You are my all,

Dearest, and I just worship you, you have been friend, sweetheart and everything to me and I will do anything you ask me to to help repay your kindness. Good night, Dearest, in Kinistino we shall be together again.

> Your honest, faithful and true,
> Jack boy

The tent was a stroke of genius. Not only did it reinforce his tragic, lonely image, part of his appeal for Jessie—but a tent had no address for mail he didn't want Polly to see, or the sudden appearance of unwanted visitors from Blaine Lake.

As Jack wrote love letters to Jessie, Polly wrote letters home, wonderfully happy ones for the first few weeks. Even later, when she realized something was seriously wrong, her letters were still cheerful. She said nothing of her suspicions to her family.

∽

In the summer of 1918, Jessie moved to Prince Albert and went to work at the Holy Family Hospital, planning, it appears, to train as a nurse in the fall. Her mother had begun to disapprove of her attachment to Jack Wilson. In Prince Albert, Jessie could see Jack without worrying about upsetting her mother.

An excerpt from Jack's letter to Jessie, July 12, 1918:

> I have just found out today that it is over 300 miles by road so even at twenty miles per hour it will take fifteen hours steady running but just as soon as I reach Prince Albert I will phone you from the New Windsor Hotel . . . I have a list of everything in the way of what I can think of that you like and will do all my shopping just before leaving so that everything will be nice and fresh for you when I get up beside you. [It is clear from the beginning of the letter that Jessie has been ill.] . . . But the Grey Dort will have to travel some cause I am so anxious to see you again . . .
>
> It has been very hot here this week, Jessie, and I was just thinking that you would be uncomfortably hot in the hospital . . . and that would tire you out even more.
>
> I do hope you are happy in the hospital, dear, I cannot bear to think of your being unhappy . . . Jessie, my love for you seems to grow more and

more all the time and you are never from my thoughts just always wondering if you are well and happy . . . I will write you on Sunday again, Dearest, then I will come myself after that and be beside my wee girl again. Now, Dearest Jessie, good night,

> Your Honest, clean and true,
> Jack boy

Polly, pregnant, suffering from the heat and lonely in a strange country, also needed Jack's understanding, but by the summer of 1918, Jack's letters and actions are those of a man completely besotted with another woman.

∽

Around this time, Jack told Jessie that his brother Alex had been killed in action. A short while later, he told Jessie that his remaining sister, "poor Isa," had also mysteriously died. While reinforcing his tragic family history, he had now cut himself off from his family.

At this time, Jack presented Jessie with the gift of a car, a second-hand Grey Dort—pretty heady stuff for a young woman in those days. Not many women had a car of their own to drive. Not many even timidly drove their husband's cars. Of course, the car would spark even more gossip, but Jack's remark that he would kiss her even if she slapped him shows the relationship was platonic.

In spite of his personal dilemma, or perhaps because of it (working long hours to avoid Polly's company), Wilson excelled in the Military Police and was offered the position of chief inspector. With pride he wrote to Jessie:

> Department of Justice,
> Military Service Branch.
> Regina, Friday 2 P.M.
> 2nd Aug. 1918

My Dearest Jessie,

I have good news for you tonight, Dearest. The boss is going to quit and I am asked today to take his place. I don't know what to do. The pay is $200 per month. Dearest Jessie, won't you come to me now if Mother is willing? It is one of the best jobs in the Province and your Jack boy would be Chief Inspector Wilson of the Dominion Police and my wee girl would be right up in Society but all the society her Jack boy wants is Jessie Patterson, the best wee friend he has in this world. This will delay me in coming to Prince Albert now, Dearest, until Tuesday or Wednesday but I will be there in lots of time for the fair.

I hope you are having a good time with the car, Jessie. I arranged with the garage men to give you the very best service and any time you want the car oiled or fixed in any way, just phone them and they will come for the car and do anything you want. I made everything all right with them. Now, Dearest, remember what you promised me about the gasoline and everything so please little girl keep your promise.

Jessie, I cannot live without you now. I just worship you, I think, so, Jessie, I am going to Blaine Lake on this trip to see Mother and then I am coming for my wee girl and take her away to love and happiness. I may not be so jolly and good-looking as other fellows, Dearest, but your Jack boy will love and honour you and do all in his power to make you the happiest wee girl on earth.

At my wages now, we will be able to afford everything that you have a mind for . . . Oh, Jessie, I don't think you know the depth of my love for you and I tell myself to be so lucky in knowing that you love me in return . . . I will wire you just as soon as I know when I can get up next week, beside my wee girl again.

Your loving and faithful,
Jack Boy

Jack couldn't resist trying to impress Jessie and fantasizing a bit about how things might be were it not for Polly, but he knew he and Jessie couldn't live together in Regina. Even if Polly went home to Scotland, or conveniently died, several people knew about her. Eileen Wismer, for one. And the Wilsons and the Laings from Hungry Hollow (later named Grand Coulee)—Thelma Wilson was an old school friend of Polly's (who had also married a John Wilson), and her mother, Mrs. Laing, was an old friend of Polly's mother. They had both visited Polly at Mrs. Wismer's. And, of course, there were the other roomers at the house. She had become quite close to Mrs. Hansen across the hall.

Wilson gave two reasons for turning down the position. He said that he felt unqualified for the job, and that he preferred a position that had opened up in Saskatoon. He requested a transfer, and it was granted. In September a new detachment would open in Saskatoon with Sub-Inspector John Wilson in charge.

As the summer wore on, Polly's pregnancy began to show, and in those days it was not seemly for women to flaunt their condition; there was still something vaguely shameful about it, having everyone know what you'd been up to. Pregnant women went out walking mostly in the evenings, on the arm of their solicitous and sheepishly proud husbands.

Polly's husband was not solicitous, nor proud, nor there to offer his arm. He was just not there, and this glaring fact was embarrassing and hurtful. When he was there, he waited until dark to take her out walking, and then always to the park, never to any public place. She'd been alone for much of the last pregnancy, and had thought this one would be so different. At least at home she'd had the children and her family and work. This time she was alone in a strange country, and achingly lonely for her children and family and friends, and faced with the increasingly obvious fact that her husband no longer loved her—and that he was, she was beginning to suspect, in love with another woman. Something was far wrong, she knew it.

But what should she do? Go home to birth another baby without a husband, and the bitter prospect of raising *three* fatherless children? No, Jack tired of things easily. She would wait and see.

One evening, Jack went out to meet some friends, leaving his tunic hanging in their room with a letter addressed in a woman's handwriting protruding from the pocket. Polly took out the letter and opened it.

It began, "Dearest Jack." Polly fell into a chair, shakily spreading the letter open on her lap. Some words leapt out at her:

And, Jack, I'm glad you are saving money for our wedding, too. Since a girl only gets married once in her life, I'd like it to be nice, though not expensive . . .

We are very busy at the hospital and the heat is terrible in the nurses' rooms. I'm glad you are coming again on Friday, your Jessie misses you . . .

Polly clamped her hand over her mouth, and the pages slithered to the floor. Marriage? To her husband? What on earth was the girl talking about? She sat for some time, just staring into space. It was all too clear that Jack knew what she meant. But they were planning to *marry*? Saving for a *wedding*? She shook her head as if she could shake loose those words that made no sense. Well, one thing was clear, she couldn't ignore it any longer.

Polly went to the bathroom and pressed a cold facecloth against her burning cheeks and neck. Then she went to the closet and pulled out the only dress still large enough, combed her hair, got a fresh handkerchief from the drawer and went out.

Mrs. Wismer and a neighbour were sitting on the cool veranda, their voices murmuring in the dusk. Moths fluttered at the screen, and the pink petunias overflowing the window boxes drenched the soft summer night with their spicy perfume. A couple walked by on the street, and the woman laughed. In the distance, a car horn honked. Everything seemed strangely vivid to Polly.

"Are you going to get a little air, Polly? It must be hot upstairs," Eileen said.

"Aye, it is, a wee bit."

Outside, she clicked the gate behind her and set off for town. He would be at the Station, that's where the policemen gathered to socialize.

ᴖ

At the Station, Wilson, his friend Conrad Read and some of the other policemen were sitting at their usual table, trading yarns about rounding up army deserters.

"And the old lady was sitting the whole time in a long black skirt in a kind of dark corner. Just as I was leaving I saw she had three feet."

"Three feet? Go on!"

"Yes. Sticking out from under her skirt, and one of them was in a big brown boot."

"No!"

"God's oath. He was hiding under Mama's skirt the whole time!" Heads turned as laughter erupted from their table.

As Wilson threw his head back, laughing uproariously, he saw Polly standing behind Con across the table. He stopped abruptly, and the men looked up and saw Polly.

"Hello, Jack," she said.

Wilson got up abruptly and walked her several tables away. He could feel the men's curious glances.

"Are you coming home soon, Jack? I need to talk to you."

"Is that all? I thought something bad must have happened."

As she was forming the words to say something bad *had* happened, he said, "You had no business coming after me. I'll see you at home." And he turned back to the table.

Polly could scarcely walk away, she felt so awkward and embarrassed with all their eyes on her. He hadn't even introduced her.

Back at the house, the veranda was empty. In desperation, Polly sought out Eileen Wismer in the big warm kitchen where she was peeling apples for pies. The two had grown close over the months, with Polly talking to Eileen about her children, showing her their letters and pictures, and taking an interest in Eileen's family. Polly slumped into a chair, her face flushed and tear-stained.

"Polly, what's the matter, dear?"

"I've thought for a long time Jack has another girl, and now I know."

Eileen dried her hands on her apron and sat down across from her.

"You mean a ladyfriend? How do you know?"

"I found a letter from her in Jack's pocket. She thinks he's saving up to marry her."

"*Marry* her? Good heavens, how could she think that?"

"I don't know!" Polly rocked from side to side in her misery, hugging her arms. "I don't know what to do. Should I go to Blaine Lake and tell this girl Jack is married?"

"I should think so. The very idea! Or at least write or phone her. Doesn't she know he's married?"

"She must not. He must not have told her." Polly fumbled for the handkerchief from her pocket and blew her nose. She was a bit calmer now. "I followed him down to the Station tonight. He was acting the fool, blethering away with a bunch of young fellows."

"Oh? I wondered where you went. Did he see you?"

"Yes, I went right up to the table. And you know he tried to pretend I was somebody he hardly knew. He didn't even introduce me. I felt so humiliated I cried all the way home." And as she relived it, tears spilled over again.

Eileen took her hand and held it. Poor little Polly. But she wasn't surprised, somehow. She'd always thought there was something underhanded about Jack Wilson.

"And he should be proud to introduce you! Did you tell those men who you were?"

"No. I felt too embarrassed. I wish I had now."

Eileen continued to hold Polly's hand in her big, warm ones.

Polly did confront Jack about the letter, asking him how Jessie could think they were getting married. She sat on the bed while Jack stood by the door, as if he couldn't wait to leave.

"I don't know how Jessie got that idea. I've been trying to break off with her but I hated to hurt her. We only got attached because I was so ill and lonely."

"Oh, I knew I should have come over sooner," Polly said. "None of this would have happened. I blame myself."

And her husband was more than willing for her to do just that.

"I will tell her," Jack said. "But you shouldn't have come after me like that." He hadn't moved from the door, and his face was pale and tight with anger. At her, she knew, for finding out how things stood.

Polly lifted her flushed and tear-wet face to look at him. She twisted and pulled at the handkerchief in her hands.

"Tell me, Jack, I have to know. Do you love her?"

He looked back at her for a long time, his face expressionless.

She didn't ask again. She didn't need to. She dropped her eyes from his, and he went out and shut the door. She listened to his steps on the stairs, the front door open. Through the open window, she heard the creaking of the wicker rocker as he sat down on the veranda. Then she smelled the smoke of his cigarette.

She got up and slowly began to undress.

Eileen Wismer said later that Polly felt "very bad" at this time, staying in her room almost all the time. She found another letter from Jessie, which clearly showed that Jack had still not told her he was married. She showed the letter to Eileen and to Mrs. Hansen across the hall, but she did nothing to advise Jessie of her existence. So, as one searing hot day followed another and the heat accumulated in that upstairs room on Rose Street, Polly Wilson waited. And endured.

Chapter xv

∼ JESSIE ∼

To Jessie, the idea of being married at age nineteen to a police inspector must have been exciting. To be told you could buy whatever you liked, to have your own car to drive, looked after by a garageman paid by your policeman friend: it was enough to turn the head of a much older woman. But she had proved when he was broke, unemployed and ill that she didn't love him for what he could give her. And Jack knew this, constantly referring to how good she had been to him, what a true friend, and how he would do anything, anything at all, to repay her kindness.

It took courage to take up with a divorced man in rural Saskatchewan in 1918. Most people frowned on it. There was, however, one person whose approval mattered desperately to Jessie:

> Holy Family Hospital
> Aug. 27/18

Dearest Jack,

Your little girl is heartbroken today. First I have had chills yesterday and today and thought I was getting Typhoid, and this morning I got a letter from Mother saying she was sorry but why couldn't I have married someone else and saved you the bother of doing what you had already done [here Jessie must be referring to Jack getting a divorce], also her worrying about me. Mother said you wanted to be married in three or four months, while, Jack, I thought you told her in September. Mother also said she told you you would have to have the papers to show—you know, and even tho' you cabled for them they couldn't possibly be here before the end of the month, could they? I didn't know what to do, Jack. Sunday I felt so happy and today I want to die. Why have we to be so unhappy when we might be so happy.

I told you something would happen, Jack, and now I think it has, alright. Mother said at the end of her letter for me to suit myself, if I knew my own mind, but she didn't say she was pleased or hoped I was happy or anything, and my heart is breaking and I don't know what to do or tell them. I don't know if I'm going home Saturday or not. I don't feel like going home when Mother feels the way she does.

I am on my half day because I am not able to do any work. Jack, will you do me a favour? Come to P.A. Saturday on the 7:15 train and stay over till Monday morning. Now, Jack, if you love me a little bit at all come, wire and let me know if you will be here. Now, Jack, I'll tell you my idea, we could be married on Sunday and you could take me down to Kinistino for a week, Jack, as the Dr. said I ought to quit for a while till I got stronger, and if you wired for those papers we could keep everything qt. till they come except to tell Elsie [Mrs. Dunlop, Jessie's cousin] if you thought best. Now, Jack dearest, I hope you don't think me awfully forward in asking you that. Do you? Now I shall wait for a wire Friday or Thursday saying if you will come. Now good-bye, Dearest. Write as soon as you get this and tell me if you still love your little nurse.

Jessie

xxxx

P.S. Write to Mother and tell her all you intended to tell her the other day, as you won't likely be in B.L. for some time.

J.P.

The lack of Jack's divorce papers made Mrs. Patterson suspicious. That, and the fact he'd told Jessie's father his wife was dead. Even if he said it because he felt they'd disapprove of a divorced man, as Jessie believed, it was still a glaring lie.

Jack now decided to resurrect the brother he'd killed off in the war. In a letter to Jessie on July 10, he referred to a cable just received from Alex from Harriem, Holland: "JUST ESCAPED FROM PRISON CAMP,

61 DAYS IN HIDING, BADLY SMASHED UP, BROKE, CABLE MONEY."
Jack told Jessie that he immediately cabled his brother five hundred
dollars. These dramatic lies always put him in a good light. Also,
Wilson's double life had stretched him financially, and the Alex story
would help explain a shortfall.

Throughout the summer, the marriage date changed with dizzying
speed, with Jack unsure what to do about Polly, and Jessie reluctant to
go through with it without the proof of Jack's divorce. A blizzard of
letters passed between Jack and Jessie:

July 20, 1918: "And, Dearest, you are not looking well . . . Cannot
we get married now and let me care for you?"

August 2, 1918: "Jessie, I cannot live without you now. I just worship
you, . . . so, Jessie, I am going to Blaine Lake to see Mother and then I
am coming for my wee girl and take her away to love and happiness."

August 5, 1918: "Now, Dearest, try and let me have two days
together to arrange everything . . . I cannot bear to think of you working hard every day and me good and able to work for us both and
make you ever so happy and comfortable. Jessie, I am just going to
worship you after we are married so you will know beforehand that
you are not going to get doing any work. I have to make breakfast
when we are at home, you make dinner and we both make supper and
I dry the dishes always."

August 12, 1918: "Jessie, these were three happy days that we
had . . . There is no use in putting it off any longer than we can help,
Dearest . . . I felt so downhearted when I waved my handkerchief to
you on Sunday when I passed the hospital in the train . . . Remember
your Jack boy is loving you with all his heart and soul and thinking of
the day coming soon when he will take your hand and lead you away
to a happy life, with your honest, clean and true, Jack Boy."

August 20, 1918: "Now I have seen Mother and everything is all
right she is *willing and glad* that we get married. Your Happy, Jack
Boy. P.S. Get your trunk ready, Dearest, I am coming for you *now*."

This constant change of plans must have driven Jessie to distraction, and in early September she went home to Blaine Lake to recover
from her illness.

Jessie's unhappiness worried her parents, as did Wilson's conflicting stories. They were also beginning to realize that wherever Jack Wilson was, there was a bottle. Jessie said he drank because of the stress of his job. But, still, he was not shaping up as the ideal son-in-law.

> Militia and Defence
> Regina, Sunday, 15th Sept. 1918
> 8:10 P.M.

My Dearest Jessie,

I got back to Regina at 6:30 A.M. this morning . . . I will get away from here on Wednesday night and be in Blaine Lake on Thursday night . . . This is the longest time we have been parted for a while and it is so lonesome without my wee girl.

Read and a bunch of men are going to Saskatoon tonight to get everything ready for me . . . It is a terrible lot of work organizing this new arrangement and of course the bulk of the work is falling on your humble Jack boy . . . but as soon as everything is going right at Saskatoon I will have very little to do there and the hours will be very short so that I will be able to spend most of the time with you Dearest. Thursday forenoon I am going to Nutana [a residential area of Saskatoon] to see about that wee cottage for us.

Jessie, I do hope we can get married on the first of the month or on the Sunday before the first. I will always try, Dearest, and do everything I can to make you happy. I love you, Jessie, with all my heart and soul and you are getting a big lonely boy who has only one real friend in this world and that is you, Dearest. I will try and pay you back for the kindness you have shown me ever since I knew you. That is from the bottom of my heart and I just feel so lonely tonight and I would give anything just to have you in my arms just now . . . I am thinking of you all the time . . . This forenoon I kept thinking about last Sunday forenoon when we were together in the car but it always cheers me up again when I think that every day brings the time nearer when we shall always be together . . .

> Your faithful and lonely,
> Jack Boy

Slamannan parish church, where Polly Hutchison married the love of her life, John Wilson, on the first day of 1908. PHOTO: LOIS SIMMIE

The Canadian Pacific Railway station in Saskatoon, Saskatchewan, as it looked when Wilson stepped off the train in July 1912. PHOTO: COURTESY OF THE SASKATOON PUBLIC LIBRARY— LOCAL HISTORY ROOM

Second Avenue, Saskatoon's main thoroughfare, in 1914. PHOTO: SASKATCHEWAN ARCHIVES BOARD

Polly Wilson and her children, Helen (Ella) and George, in 1913. PHOTO: COURTESY OF LYNN HUDSON

The Royal North West Mounted Police headquarters and training school on the outskirts of Regina, Saskatchewan. PHOTO: RCMP MUSEUM, REGINA, SASKATCHEWAN

Top: *The Blaine Lake railway station in 1913.*

Left: *The village of Blaine Lake in 1915, the year John Wilson and the Patterson family arrived.*

Bottom: *The livery stable purchased by John Patterson in July 1915.*

Jack Wilson on duty in the Blaine Lake district. This photograph is believed to have been taken by Jessie Patterson. No picture of Jessie Patterson is available.

PHOTO: COURTESY OF LYNN HUDSON

Eileen Wismer's boarding house at 2039 Rose Street, Regina. PHOTO: FRANK ANDERSON

The burned-out Grey Dort car. The photo was taken by Isaac Peters, a nearby farmer, on September 28, 1918.

Knox Presbyterian manse, the scene of a late-night wedding on September 29, 1918.

Chapter XVI

✌ A DECISION IS REACHED ✍

Jack Wilson moved to Saskatoon on September 17, 1918, in charge of a subdivision of the Military Police, with a total of thirty-four men under him. He left Polly behind, and another hiatus began. Polly waited and worried and tried to write optimistic letters home. Better to tell them how well Jack was doing, what an important job he had—she knew people didn't think him capable of that—and to make plans for her move to Saskatoon and the arrival of the children. Better to keep the heartache to herself. She'd caused her family enough worry already, but, oh, what she wouldn't give for a talk with Lizzie!

Polly kept to her room now. She had enjoyed writing at the dining-room table, or reading and knitting on the veranda. She liked the homey smells coming from the kitchen, Eileen's cheerful steps on the stairs, boarders stopping to chat. But all that friendly domestic bustle made her feel worse now, and she wrote in her room at the small table by the window. Her life up to now had been so full of work and family, and she missed that. No one here needed her. Now the days were agonizingly long and idle, slowly gathering like a scream inside her.

Eileen's bouquets, which brightened Polly's room, had changed over the months; sweet peas and cosmos and baby's-breath giving way to spicy autumnal asters, dahlias, marigolds. The breezes that lifted the white lace curtains in and out, as if the house were breathing, were suddenly cool, tangy with autumn. And sometimes at night she wakened to the haunting sound of geese flying over, gabbling excitedly, like souls on Judgement Day. In the morning she watched the children going to school. She had missed little Ella's first days at school.

In Saskatoon, Jack Wilson now had another reason to worry. Polly was just a short train ride away. Her sudden arrival from Scotland and her appearance at the Station that night had made him edgy. He could blame only himself, leaving his jacket with the letter out in plain sight. Had he wanted her to find it? It was hard to know any more. He was drinking too much—he had been for quite a while—and his mind wasn't as sharp as it should be. Well, in his situation, who wouldn't drink?

Wilson had indeed become a serious drinker. At this time he was seen drunk in uniform on a train by a member of the RNWMP, and since Wilson was drinking or at Blaine Lake half the time, his men in Saskatoon had no one to tell them what to do. Conrad Read, a close friend, moved with him from the Regina office. So had a man called Ramsden, and the three were great boozing buddies. Wilson and possibly Read were also involved in some kind of underhanded activity to do with collecting Military Service Act fines from army deserters.

Jessie was now just a two-hour drive away. She saw him often, but still pressured him about his divorce papers:

Blaine Lake,
September 15, 7:30 P.M.

My Dearest Jack,

I have been fairly busy this week, Jack, and Mother and I have had a few talks. Oh, Jack, I do wish you could have been here today. There is something I do want to ask you, I have often asked it before but this will be the last time and, Jack, as soon as you can you will come over, won't you?

Mother has not been very well, had another heart attack Friday night. I managed to stop it before she got very bad and Dr. said I did very well. Somehow, Jack, he, the doctor, seems to have changed his opinion of me as he spoke the other night as tho' I were some, I don't know what. I'd like to know what he thinks, so ever since when I meet him, I merely say, "How-do-you-do," and keep going on. Oh, I can't say what I would like to about that but what do you suppose he thinks?

I am feeling fine . . . but the pain in my lungs is still bad. Mother is having the Dr. examine me to see if they are affected or not. Just think, Jack, I only have two weeks left before I start back to the *Hospital* to nurse again. I hope it won't be as hard this time as it was the last . . . And I want to tell you, Johnny boy, that next year if we are living you are to take me out shooting on the 15th of September no matter what you are doing or where.

Always yours,
Nurse Patterson

P.S. If my letter seems strange, Jack, I'll explain why when I see you.

The question she had to ask him one last time was surely about his divorce, since her mother was turning against the marriage because he hadn't produced the papers. Even Jessie must have wondered if he was really free to marry her. How could she not? Jessie's letter seems aimed at forcing Jack into a firm commitment; she knew he worried about her and hated her working at the hospital. If that was the purpose of the letter, it worked stunningly well. He would not see his Jessie go back to work.

A week after receiving Jessie's letter, he called two of his men, James Martin and Jim Matthews, into his office at the Armoury and asked them to meet him in the washroom. The mystified pair did as they were told.

"Well, boys," Wilson said, producing a flask of Scotch whisky from under his tunic and passing it to Martin, "have a drink on me."

Martin took the flask. "What are we celebrating, if I may ask? Are we getting a raise in pay?"

Wilson's laugh echoed in the bare, high-ceilinged room. "No. Better than that. I just came from the doctor and he gave me the go ahead to get married."

"You mean you have to ask a doctor if you want to get married?" Matthews asked.

"Well, I've been wanting to get married for a long time, but the doctor wouldn't give me a clean bill of health because of my lungs. But they're all clear now, he said, so I'm going ahead with it."

"That's good news. So when is the big day?"

"This weekend. Friday night or Saturday, if we can get a minister."

"Here's to your happiness, sir," Martin said. And all drank to the happy occasion.

Wilson always wrote to Jessie as soon as possible after seeing her. The following letter is undated. Subsequent events put the date at September 22.

Saskatoon, Monday 7 P.M. 1918

My Dearest Jessie,

Well, I suppose you have heard all about the noise I was the cause of this morning in B.L. I slept in until 6:35 A.M. and got up and hurried down to the barracks. My Dukobor refused to come for breakfast so I went back to the hotel and had mine and went down to the barracks with the car. I saw there was going to be a scrap with the woman so I ordered her outside and she refused so we had to pull her out and after she got on the sidewalk she kicked me all over the body and I did not want to abuse her 'cause I was sorry for her in a way, as she wanted to undress and of course I would not let her, but I was forced at the end to put handcuffs on her. She was as strong as an ox. She tore a big piece of flesh right out of my left hand with her teeth, right clean into the bone, and it was terribly sore all the way down in the car and bled all the way to Saskatoon. I had to go to the doctor here and get it fixed. I think I am black and blue all over with her kicking, and some places are pretty sore. She is a pure devil.

The Duk himself did not have nearly so much game in him. He was a trifle angry at first and took all his clothes off, but when he realized he had to go to Saskatoon anyway even with no clothes, he changed his mind and put everything on but his boots. He gave a little trouble coming down but nothing serious. I will always be afraid of women after this I think, so I will always be very quiet with you, Jessie.

I have been terribly busy all day today. There is so much work to do. I am going away out now to get *our marriage licence* and go to Nutana to look for *our* rooms, I have already been to the Agent and he thinks he will get us a nice house very quickly. I told him to put an advt. in the paper if he considered it necessary . . .

It was real cold coming down this morning . . . I was wishing I could see you this morning, Dearest, before I went away, and I am going to try somehow to get up on Wednesday night, so if you hear a noisy bunch arrive you will know who has come. I was thinking of going down to the Hospital tomorrow and try and get 2 or 3 crippled soldiers and bring them up for a good time, if I manage to let the O.C. give them a pass overnight I will have to ask you to help me to give them a good time and I know you will do that, Dearest, to cheer up the poor fellows. I am a little afraid it is going to rain or snow it is so cold tonight, it was threatening rain when I came in tonight. I do hope it keeps off and that I don't have to go to Regina on Wednesday so that I can come and see you . . . If I get the crippled boys I could not travel very fast with them in case of jolting their wounds. I hope, dearest, you are feeling well and none the worse of the week-end trip and your mother also. I have been so sorry since that I scared her in turning that corner I will never forgive myself for that. I thought about it every time I turned a corner coming down this forenoon.

Now, little girl, I am going to get our licence and try and get our rooms, then I am coming back to work until late so that I will have everything done up for Wednesday. Sunday will soon be here when we shall be parted no more until Death comes. Oh, Jessie, the more I see of you the higher you raise in my estimation. On Saturday night, Dearest, when we were talking I was just thinking how hard I would have to try to make you happy and make myself worthy of your Love.

> Your Loving, kind and true
> Jack boy

The same evening he wrote to Jessie, he also wrote this letter:

> Militia and Defence
> Saskatoon, Monday, September 22

Dear Polly,

I thought I would get home on Sunday night or this morning, but everything seems to be upside down in here. I got in from Rosetown on Sunday at 2:30 P.M. so I am going to remain in Saskatoon until tomorrow forenoon then I have to go to Humbolt and if it is not too cold for you would you do the packing down there and leave the trunks at Regina until we get settled here in Saskatoon. I have been to the Real Estate Agent here and asked him to try and get us a nice 3 roomed house near work and I think that will be a lot better for you than a room.

Now if you take the 8:20 A.M. train CPR from Regina to Colonsay I will meet you there on Friday afternoon at 1:15 P.M. I shall have a livery car and we can go on to Humbolt together then come in to Saskatoon after I get finished there and get settled down here then send for our trunks. Your grip would hold enough clothes to keep both of us going until say about Tuesday of next week when we would be settled down. I would come down if you don't care to travel alone but everything is in such a mess and I must also get to Humbolt and Wadena so that would let us get quicker together again and, Polly, your old man is missing you and I know you are wearying also. I think you will like this place better than Regina, Polly, and I won't have to go out except very seldom. It has been terribly cold and my new coat came in very handy.

You will need to wear warm clothes, Polly, as it is cold driving but it is not so very bad in the car and that will be better than you waiting for me at Regina and wearying your life out. Mrs. Wismore [sic] will keep our trunks until Monday or Tuesday and we can wire her when we are ready for them. But, Polly, you better buy a new big one in place of the old one even if it does cost a bit as it is liable to go to pieces and just have labels on them all ready so that the drayman can just call for them and ship them. The Government will pay the expenses.

I will close now as I might miss the mail if I don't. I will also write a night letter and have them send it tonight in case I am too late for the mail.

> I remain,
> Your Loving Husband,
> Jack

He did take the returned soldiers to Blaine Lake for a party later that week. Drinking with other people helped to take his mind off Polly's arrival.

In several letters to Jessie, Jack mentioned a red coat of Jessie's, purchased in Saskatoon and left for alterations, probably part of her wedding outfit. And Wilson, like any happy groom, was making wedding preparations of his own. He asked where he could buy a marriage licence. He rented rooms for him and Jessie until that "wee cottage" materialized.

And, in one of the little towns or country stores on his travels, Jack Wilson bought a shovel.

Chapter XVII

RED ROSES FOR POLLY

It was a time of waiting. The still, autumn days now smelled of earth and smoke, and late red poppies glowed in the ragged gardens. One by one their crimson petals fell to the ground. The days were closing in.

And then the letter came.

"Oh, I must pack right away, Mrs. Wismer. Jack has got us a house in Saskatoon."

"Well, that must be good news, I'm sure. It will be nice for you to be settled in your own place again."

"I must write the children today and tell them they'll be coming over soon." Polly folded the letter. "I hope my sister Elizabeth will travel with them."

"Oh, that would be lovely for you, wouldn't it?" Mrs. Wismer tried to feel glad for Polly. She was such a nice little person; much too good for the likes of him.

"I'll be able to send for my sewing machine. I've missed it so much."

Polly started to take things slowly out of the closet. The truth was she didn't feel as happy as she should have; she felt, in fact, uneasy.

While she packed her things and Jack's, Mrs. Hansen from across the hall stopped in to bring Polly two farewell gifts, a fine black leather handbag and a gold brooch. Polly was touched: by the gifts, which were lovely, and by Mrs. Hansen's kindness. People here had been very good to her, and she would miss them.

"I'll write to you," she said.

"I just hope everything will go well for you, Polly." And Polly knew Mrs. Hansen was thinking about Jessie Patterson.

"I'm sure things will be better now, with the children coming and all," Polly said.

Later the same day, two trunks, neatly packed, strapped and labelled, stood on the landing. Jack had said they'd send for them. She appreciated that, since being in the family way made everything harder. Not that she'd have to lift them, but still, it was nice to travel light.

The next morning she withdrew all her money from the bank—three hundred dollars. She would deposit it in Saskatoon till she knew how things were going to turn out. She wondered about Jessie. Did she know about Polly now? Jack hadn't said, but surely since he'd asked her to come, he had given Jessie up. And he said in the letter he was missing her.

Jack phoned early Friday morning to tell her to come to Saskatoon instead of Colonsay, and which train to take, since there were twenty-seven trains a day into Saskatoon. He would be there to meet her at four o'clock.

"You write now, Polly. You hear?" Since Eileen Wismer couldn't get away, she'd asked Mrs. Hansen to see Polly off on the train.

"Oh, I will, don't you doubt it. You know I like writing letters." They'd often commented at the house what a faithful letter writer Polly was.

Mrs. Wismer helped Polly on with her suit jacket. "Such beautiful wool," she said. "And to think you made it yourself. You've got your money somewhere safe, have you?"

Polly nodded. "Pinned right here." She patted a spot above her left breast, and the money inside crackled.

"I'll miss you, Polly."

"And I'll never forget how kind you've been. I'm going to make you something nice as soon as I get my machine." She felt in her pocket. Yes, she had the pattern she wanted to look at on the train. A pattern for a dress for little Ella.

"Don't you be thinking about sewing for me. You're going to have your hands full when those children get here. All of them." Mrs. Wismer patted Polly's arm, and they both laughed.

"I wish I could go with you to the station, but someone is coming to look at your room."

Polly hoped whoever it was would be happier than she had been in that room.

⌒

As they waited for the train, Polly told Mrs. Hansen that she hoped the children would arrive in time for Christmas and Hogmanay, Scottish New Year's Eve. Many Scots didn't make much of Christmas, viewing it as a papist celebration, but the children loved it. It was Jack's and her eleventh anniversary, too, on the first day of the new year.

They passed a man selling corsages, and Polly stopped. "Oh, look. Aren't they lovely?"

"Well, why not treat yourself? It's a special day, after all."

It was sinfully extravagant, but Mrs. Hansen was right, wasn't she? She must look on this as a new beginning.

"I'll have that one, please. With the red roses and white carnation."

"That will be lovely on your suit," Mrs. Hansen said.

Later, in the swaying washroom on the train, Polly pinned it to her shoulder. The money crackled as she did so. The corsage looked just right; it added colour to her cheeks.

And this time, as the train gathered speed, jarring her about in the tiny washroom, she knew one thing for sure: this time her husband would be there to meet her.

∼

The bell tinkled in Wheatley's Jewellery Store, and Wilfred Sales put down his jewellery tweezers and hurried out to wait on the policeman standing by the counter. If he hadn't been in uniform, Wilfred might have worried that this pale, nervous man intended to rob the store.

"Yes, sir. What can I do for you this fine morning?"

His customer cleared his throat and smiled, a smile that didn't reach his grey-blue eyes.

"I want to buy a marriage licence, please."

"Ah, a marriage licence." That explained it. It was always the men who were nervous about getting married. Never the ladies, who thought of nothing else since they gave each other imaginary tea parties, dandling their dollies on their laps. "Well, you've come to the right place. I'll be happy to get you a marriage licence. Misery likes company you know," he said, trying to set his customer at ease.

As he spoke, he bustled to the back of the store and pulled out a narrow oak drawer, one of many in the back wall, then returned with a form which he placed on the counter. "Yes indeedy, not many of us escape the holy bonds."

"I beg your pardon?" said the man. A bit of colour was returning to his long, craggy face. A Scotchman, by his accent. No use trying to sell him a decent ring.

"The holy bonds of matrimony. Ensnare us all in the end." Wilfred grinned cheerfully, showing two gleaming gold teeth. "Your name, sir?"

"John Wilson."

"Marital status? Silly, but they make us ask. Can't have people running around with two or three—"

"Single." Wilson's voice croaked a bit, then he added, "Bachelor."

Wilfred stood a moment with the pen poised in his small white hand. Really, this was the least happy-looking groom he'd seen in a long while. Ah, well, you never knew, shotgun wedding maybe.

"Bachelor," said Wilfred, filling in the appropriate blank. "And the lady's name?"

"Miss Jessie Patterson."

Wilfred filled in the name, wrote "Spinster" with a flourish and, marking a blank line with a neat X, swivelled the licence around for Wilson's signature. Wilson signed on the designated line, his narrow hand trembling slightly. The sprawling signature was large, the ink very black.

"There. They do make it easy for us, don't they? A little too easy I sometimes wonder." He took the five-dollar bill Wilson handed him, punched the cash register open and gave him four dollars change. "And will you be needing a wedding ring?" He waved his hand over the glass-topped showcase, where the autumn sun lay warm on all manner of gold jewellery: pocket watches, tie pins, money clips, rings.

"No."

"A nice gift for the bride then?" he asked, without much hope. "We have some lovely—"

"No."

Wilfred raised his eyebrows only a fraction. "Ah well, then." He came out from behind the counter to see the nervous groom out, thrusting out his hand at the door. "Good luck to you, sir, and to your future bride."

"Oh, yes. Thank you."

John Wilson's hand was very cold.

Outside, with the marriage licence crackling in his shirt pocket and his tunic buttoned securely over it, Wilson drew a deep, careful breath. Aware that the clerk was standing just inside the window, watching him, he started purposefully down the street.

Turning abruptly, he headed down the street to where he'd parked the Grey Dort. Polly would soon be arriving, and he had to get something to eat. It was long past noon, and he needed to keep his strength up. He bumped into a large woman just coming out of Albert's Café but he didn't apologize; seemed, in fact, not to see her at all.

"Hmmmph," she said aloud, turning to look at him. "And him a policeman, too."

∾

As Wilson ate his late meal, Polly looked out at the new country she'd seen so little of since her arrival. The train clacked and lurched along, passing straw-coloured fields busy with farmers and hayracks and those big machines that looked like prehistoric animals ambling over the plains. Sometimes a farmer paused to wave at the train. Polly waved back. The land seemed to go on forever as did the immense blue sky studded with cotton-batting clouds.

She thought about having a house again. She hadn't seen anything here as nice as the stone house she'd left behind, but whatever John had found would be fine. And they could manage somehow until their things were sent from home.

She looked at the pattern for the wean's dress. Ella would look so sweet in it. She would cut it generously since Ella would have grown since spring. And she'd hand turn some nappies and knit some soakers for the new bairn. And make a shirt for Georgie, so he wouldn't feel left out. Surely Jack would love the new bairn when it arrived. He'd been so good with wee George. Everyone talked about it and said they'd never seen a father like him. He didn't take much interest in Ella, but that was only because he didn't know her.

She would put this hard time behind her—they both would—and start to live again as a family. You just had to forgive and go on, that's all there was to it. Especially when you had children.

"Saskatoon! Saskatoon! Next stop Saskatoon!" called the navy-uniformed conductor, swaying slowly through the coach. "Please take your baggage and parcels with you. Saska—" The door at the far end of the rocking coach cut off his voice. The seven-hour trip had gone faster than last time. Was it really only a few months ago that she'd travelled here to meet him?

Polly put on her cape, gathering her purse and gloves from the green plush seat into her lap. The train was slowing down, hissing and jarring and knocking people about. As the platform appeared, she leaned forward, looking for him.

For a moment she thought he hadn't come, and then she saw him, standing against the station wall, almost pressing into it. He looked small and pale. He wasn't over the effects of that bout with TB yet. She would fatten him up when she had a chance to cook again, everything he liked; cock-a-leekie soup, tatties, cullen skink.

Polly was the first one off the train.

Chapter XVIII

↜ IT'S GETTING DARK ↝

Jack did not drive Polly straight to the house. He had to go out Rosthern way on business, he said, and she might as well come along for the ride. And since it was so nice to be actually going somewhere with him, she didn't complain. The house would be there when they got back.

Polly was hungry, but Jack seemed in a hurry to get out in the country, so they stopped at a small grocery store where she bought some fruit to eat in the car. Then they went into Cairns Store and walked around it for a bit, but Polly bought only some postcards to send to the children.

Polly had hardly been for a car ride since she arrived, except for that long drive to Regina the first day. It was lovely, riding along, seeing the fields and the harvesting and the duck-filled sloughs close up. There was a wonderful crop that year, even a stranger could tell that, the grain standing thick and heavy, or sheafed into big generous stooks, as Jack called them. Where it was cut and still lay in thick curving rows, it glistened and shone as if waiting for Rumpelstiltskin to turn it into gold. A mellow golden light lay over everything, the wildflowers in the ditches, the silvery wolf willow, the telephone poles and wires looping along beside the road. It was all so meltingly lovely, this rich autumn day in her new country.

Jack did not say much, but as on that trip to Regina, he kept reaching under the seat for a bottle of whiskey, downing several large swallows each time. She didn't say anything. She knew he must have a lot to think about in his new job, so she just enjoyed the moment, the sights and sounds and smells and bird song.

Not far out of Saskatoon there was a popping sound and the car went out of control; one of the rear tires was flat. While Jack changed the tire, Polly got out and walked down the road a bit, admiring the few wildflowers still blooming by the road, inhaling their faint perfume. It mingled with the scent of the roses in her corsage, and the spicy fragrance of white carnation, the stronger of the two. She touched their petals, soft and dewy, like a baby's cheek.

On their way again, they saw a big brown rabbit bounding along in a stubble field. It was lovely to see it running free, zigzagging through the swath. Jack stopped, leapt out of the car and shot the rabbit. Polly hadn't even noticed the shotgun in the back. He walked back holding the dead rabbit upside-down, blood running from its long soft ears. He threw it in the back beside the shovel. Then he gave Polly the gun and showed her how to hold it beside her in case some geese flew over and he needed it quickly. She wouldn't mind having a goose to cook, but she wished he hadn't shot the rabbit.

A long time later, he suddenly spoke up.

"It's too late now to do my work at Rosthern today. I thought we would go to Blaine Lake instead."

"Blaine Lake? Why?" She went suddenly cold.

"To go there and explain things to Jessie."

"You haven't done that yet?"

"No, I thought we should go together. When she sees you, she'll know it's no use."

Well, maybe that would be best. Let the girl see that Jack had a wife in the family way, almost six months along. And Polly would be sure Jessie knew about the other bairns, too. And she had to admit to herself that she was curious to see this young woman who was planning to marry her husband. Poor lassie, none of this was her fault. Polly understood their becoming attached while he was lonely and sick. If she could not understand loneliness, who could? And she had had the children.

And so Polly leaned back and let Jack have his thoughts to himself. This would be hard enough for him. No need for her to go on about it and make it worse. But now she understood why he was driving slower and slower.

"Is it a long way to Blaine Lake?"

"It's not far now."

They were practically crawling along, as if Jack was looking for something. She ate one of the apples she'd bought in Saskatoon. Best to say nothing.

Then he suddenly drove off on a faint trail to the left, and Polly hung on to the door as they bounced over the rough ground. They stopped not far from a culvert.

"Geese," Jack said, getting out and going around to her side of the car and lifting out the gun.

And geese there were, flying in to feed in the field beside the road. And then they were overhead, their honking loud in the stillness. Jack aimed and shot. One spiralled erratically to the earth quite a way off, then threshed along for a long time, wounded. She got out of the car and walked behind him in that direction, but he turned suddenly and said it was too far, they'd better get on.

"I hope it won't die," Polly said, as they walked back to the car, which was hidden from the road by some bushes. It was dusk now, and would soon be dark. They could hear a car passing by on the road, then silence. Polly was hungry.

"Don't you think we'd better get on, Jack? It's getting dark."

"Yes, I suppose we'd better get it over with."

They walked back to the car where Jack put the car robe over her side of the seat, then took his topcoat from the back seat and put it on. Yes, it was cooler now, Polly thought, as she climbed in and gratefully settled down. She was feeling a wee bit tired from the long day, and the bairn inside was kicking her. They'd both be fine as soon as she ate. It was so quiet there they might have been all alone in the world.

Jack hadn't moved from her side of the car. He was very pale, standing there in dim light, perspiration on his upper lip and forehead. Why was he looking at her like that? Polly felt a sudden start of dread.

Jack still had the gun. Why didn't he put it away? It was getting too dark to shoot. But he was raising the gun again.

She looked up, but there were no geese. She turned back and looked straight into the shotgun's double barrel, inches from her face.

"No, Jack, *don't*!"

At the loud explosion, the good, generous heart of Polly Wilson stopped beating. The boy child inside her struggled. It took a little longer for his heart to stop.

Chapter XIX

⌒ IT WAS AN ACCIDENT ⌒

It was terrible. He had no idea it would be so terrible. The top of her head gone, blood spurting everywhere, then just pouring out, like water from a broken jug. Blood everywhere. Her blue suit a sopping maroon; not only blood, bits of brain and bone and skin sticking to everything, his hands and face, his dispatch case, the windshield. Why in God's name had he shot her in the head? Why did he do it? He hadn't really meant to, had he? At least he never wanted this, to hear that horrible gurgling "aaahh" sound coming out of her throat—Oh, God, was she still alive? No, no, she couldn't be, her head, that overpowering stench of blood and gunpowder, and him suddenly sick all down the side of the car, a geyser of vomit. The awful panic, the smell, the sound of his panting breath, his own voice in his ear. *Go somewhere . . . tell somebody . . . it was an accident, it could have been, she wasn't used to handling a gun, she could have. Get in the car, drive somewhere and hand her over. Get away from her. No, first wash in the bit of water in the slough, the blood drying satin smooth like fish scales . . . and the dispatch case, sodden and sticky in the front seat . . . never mind it, get going, that's better, get some air.*

But she kept falling over. What was left of her head lolled on his shoulder like some ghastly parody of a courting couple. He turned fast onto the trail going west, then south again on the road to Saskatoon.

It's almost dark, thank God. Be careful, slow down, no use in killing youself too. It's done now and you can't undo it. You can't see her, thank God, just feel her, limp, sticky. Push her away, stop the car and think.

Dr. Langlois, the coroner at Marcelin, he knows you from the Beerekoff case. He'll help. Just go there and explain about the accident. It could have happened to anybody. No. Who is going to believe that when you marry Jessie tomorrow?

Jessie. Just hang onto the thought of Jessie and you'll get through this. What would she think if she could see you now? Well, she can't, and please God she will never know what you had to go through for her.

He pulled into a weedy trail, and as he turned around, Polly suddenly fell sideways onto the dispatch case and stuck to it, matter running out of her head. He pushed her up against the door and vomited again in the weeds by the car. Crickets and frogs, something rustling through the weeds, like any normal prairie night, reassuring till he turned back and the moonlight caught in her eyes as if she was watching him.

He turned back the way he came, jouncing over the rough road. Finally he stomped on the brake by the culvert and threw open the door and she pitched out into the grass, onto her back with her feet on the running board, her skirt up above her knees. Her features all awry now, eyes staring up at the moon. An owl hooted in a nearby tree, and he nearly jumped out of his skin.

Calm down, take a deep breath. You can't change it now. And maybe you wouldn't if you could. Think of Jessie, how you always said you would do anything in the world to make her happy.

❧

After a long time, when the nausea and shaking stopped, he got up and took the blood-soaked grey car robe from the front seat and threw it over that dreadful staring face. He got the shovel from the back of the car and began to dig under the culvert.

It was terrible digging under there, all bent over. Two hours later, weak and exhausted, he stopped. How would he ever dig it deep enough? He wanted to be in Blaine Lake before dawn to avoid meeting threshers on the road. When he went to get his gloves from under the back seat, he found the bottle the boys had left there Wednesday night on the trip to Blaine Lake. That seemed like a year ago. He drank what was left and was sick again. Finally, he felt a little stronger. Something brushed past in the rushes around the slough. A rush of wings as an owl swooped, a startled cry. He couldn't stop to rest. Threshers would be going to work at the crack of dawn.

And finally, ages later, he dragged her there, the moon his only witness.

It was almost dawn when, checking around one last time, he drove back down the trail to the main road. When he reached it, he stopped and sat a few moments, thinking. Should he go back? What if he'd missed something? No, it was getting light, and he didn't want to meet anyone if he could help it.

He turned onto the main road, and as he approached the culvert, he sped up, suddenly desperate to escape that place. But, driving fast with no lights, he glanced down beside the culvert, and a front wheel caught in the soft earth of the bank . . .

Chapter xx

⤳ THAT DAMNED CAR BURNED DOWN ON ME ⤳

Isaac Neufeldt stood at the kitchen window waiting for the coffee to perk. He'd finished breakfast, and thick beef sandwiches, his mid-morning lunch, were made and waiting on the cupboard. It was going to be another good day, the sun just rising in a pale morning sky clear as a bell. If he didn't miss his guess, some of the boys would already be over at Pete's place. They should finish up there today, and tomorrow they'd start on his. They'd had perfect threshing weather so far; there were only his and his brother John's places left, and they'd got an early start.

He was just turning back to take the coffee off when he saw a stranger stumbling up the lane towards the house. He was in a uniform of some kind, weaving a bit, and white as a sheet. When Isaac stepped out on the back steps, he saw black smoke down by the culvert. When he looked back, the man was bent over, puking into the lilac bush. Isaac started toward him.

"Have you got trouble?" he called.

The man straightened up and wiped his mouth on the back of his hand, then pulled a handkerchief from his pocket and cleaned off his hand with it. He was dirty and wild-eyed.

"The damned car burned on me. Can I get a drink of water?"

"Yes, sure. The pump's right over here. How did it happen?" Now he was close enough, Isaac smelled vomit and smoke on him. A whiff of liquor, too.

"I was driving to Blaine Lake and a fire started in the back of the car. I seen the slough and thought there was water in it, so I drove over the grade there, hoping to put it out."

The stranger's hands shook. His clothes were covered with dust, the back of his right hand was bleeding, and he looked as nervous as a cat on a hot griddle. Isaac pumped him a cold drink of water and he drank the whole dipperful in a few gulps, then lurched back to the lilac bush and chucked it up. He kept on heaving for a bit but nothing more came up.

"Sorry," he said when he was finished. "I swallowed too much smoke, and my stomach's kind of touchy."

Isaac had his own ideas about what the stranger had swallowed too much of but it wasn't for him to say, and the man was in trouble.

"I'll go on down with you and see what we can do." Isaac started down the lane at a good clip. "Where were you headed when it happened?"

"I was following a lead on some army deserters hiding out up north of Blaine Lake. There's no use hurrying. The car's a goner." He seemed a little better after being sick.

And he was right. When they got down there, the car was pretty well burned out. Wild zigzag tracks in the bank showed where he'd tried to get back on the road. The front and back seats were on the ground with the upholstery all gone, just the springs. All the wood parts were burned—the steering wheel just spokes—the hood up and engine black, the windshield broken. It was a Grey Dort and sitting on an angle, the front wheel broken from the fall over the grade. There was a straw suitcase spattered with something dark on the ground near the car, and Isaac moved it away in case a stray spark caught it.

The man, who hadn't told Isaac his name, picked up a shovel from beside the car and started shovelling dirt on the back tires. He still looked sick as a dog. Isaac didn't see much point in what he was doing, what good were the tires when the car was done, like saving the shoes on a dead horse, but maybe it made him feel better to be doing something.

Then the boys from the threshing crew arrived, stopping the car on the road and stumbling down the bank to the burning car.

Pete Loewen whistled. "Well, would you look at that! Isn't that something?"

"Yes, and I just got it last spring," the man said, getting another shovel full of dirt from under the culvert. It was funny in a way, since the weeds and grass under there were a good foot and a half high, but Isaac didn't think too much of it with everything else going on. Then his brother John arrived, driving his car in on the trail and stopping not far from the burning car. John came over then to talk to him.

"I know that man," he told Isaac. "He came to the house Wednesday night for some gas. He had four other fellows in the car with him."

While they were just standing around, starting to think about the work they weren't getting done, Isaac heard Henry Williams ask how the car got there.

"I was on my way to Blaine Lake, and just before the culvert I smelled fire in the back. When I turned to look, I went over the culvert."

"It's a wonder you landed on your wheels," Isaac Peters said.

"Yes, I couldn't believe it myself. I sure was going some."

"So the fire started in the back, then?"

"Yes. They ran the tank over when I got her filled before I left Saskatoon around three this morning."

Now that was funny, too, Isaac thought. The man had told him a different story. And the fire had started in the front, the boys all agreed later. The back was hardly scorched. The fellow must think they were stupid, he thought, but they just put it down to his drinking. The other boys said later they thought he was drunk, or partly drunk. And you could see where he'd been sick on the ground and on the car before he came up to the house. He never told them his name, and they hated to ask. Maybe he had a reason, him being a policeman and drunk when he had the accident. Henry Funk moved some shotgun shells that were lying on the ground pretty close to the car. The shotgun was there, and he moved that, too. And Pete Loewen moved a straw suitcase, speckled with something red.

"I shot some geese," the man said. "They got burned in the back of the car." And he kept on shovelling dirt on the back tires.

Now that was another peculiar thing. There wasn't any smell of burned feathers or cooked goose, and they would've smelled that.

Then John Neufeldt offered to drive him to Blaine Lake, but first the Neufeldts and the policeman went to John's house for breakfast.

"So what were you going to Blaine Lake for so early in the morning?" John's wife asked the man, after he'd washed up and they were sitting at the table. John's kids were all agog at having breakfast with a policeman.

"I have to be in court there this morning," he said. He was one of those police who rounded up the soldiers, he explained. Then, as an afterthought, he said, "I'm looking for some army deserters up north, too."

Once during breakfast he got up from the table and went out in the yard and threw up again. It spoiled everybody's appetite, and Albert clutched his throat and rolled his eyes, making the girls laugh. When he came back in, the policeman started shaking like a leaf and said he was "awful cold." John's wife said it was probably the shock he'd had and John loaned him his overcoat for the ride. Isaac was sorry he hadn't thought to offer him a coat at his place, but his mind was on getting to the car.

It was funny, somehow, Isaac thought. The whole darn thing was funny.

Later that day Isaac Peters went down and took some pictures of the car.

John Neufeldt took his children along on the drive to Blaine Lake. The car was still enough of a novelty to be exciting, and they never turned down the chance of a ride.

First, they all went down to the car where the policeman picked up the shotgun and suitcase and shovel. He put the suitcase on the floor in the back seat of the car, and then the four children, Albert, Henry, Agnes and Katie, who'd got out to look at the car, piled back in again.

It was a beautiful drive and, except for the children in the back seat, an almost completely silent one. Neufeldt's passenger hardly said a word, except to explain that he always carried a shovel in case he had to dig himself out or was stuck and had to get the car pulled out.

In the back, Katie Neufeldt pointed at the straw suitcase. "Look," she said, her voice low so they couldn't hear her over the sound of the motor. "What does that look like?"

"Blood," Albert whispered in her ear.

"What?" asked Agnes. "What about it?"

"It looks like blood on there." Katie pointed again at the spray of bright red spots on the light straw side.

"It is," Albert said. "It for damn sure is blood." And they laughed and started poking each other.

"Ask him," said Kate.

"No. You," Agnes said.

But then she did lean over and said to the man, "What's this red stuff that looks like blood all over the suitcase?

He looked kind of mad and, reaching over, took the suitcase into the front with him.

"It's from the geese," he said.

༚

In Blaine Lake, Jack asked Neufeldt to drop him off at the hotel, and gave him ten dollars for the ride.

"And here, you can have the shovel. I don't have any more use for it," he said. Neufeldt wondered why not; he'd surely have another car to drive, but he decided not to ask in case the policeman changed his mind about the shovel, which was brand new.

Then he took off the coat he'd borrowed. "Thanks for the use of it," he said, and picking up the suitcase and gun, he went up the steps and into the hotel.

Alex Armstrong looked up when Jack walked into the lobby, smelling of smoke and vomit, and looking as if he'd been dragged behind the car all the way from Saskatoon.

"My damned car burned down on me," Jack said, and he went into the washroom. He took the gun and suitcase in with him, which was odd, Alex thought. He was a bit relieved when Jack came back out and headed off to the Pattersons.

Chapter XXI

TILL DEATH DO US PART

The Reverend Wylie Clark hung his robe in the vestment cupboard and slipped on a cardigan sweater. Then, after turning off the lights in the Knox Presbyterian Church, he walked next door to the manse. It was a chilly night, with drizzling rain, more like November than late September. The manse looked cheery from outside, with the warm light from the piano windows. The dining-room lights were on, too. It was a sunroom, really, almost all windows, and was his favourite room. Inside he could see Agnes bent over the table, placing a bowl of asters in the centre. It was a picture to warm a man's heart on a chilly fall night. The pungent tang of wood smoke rose from the chimney. She must have lit the fire he'd laid earlier. That would be nice for the wedding.

The wedding. He turned on his heel, went back into the church and came out with a book in his hand. He knew the wedding ceremony by heart but people still felt more comfortable if he read it, or at least had the book in front of him. It made it more official.

"Not here yet?" he called, as he came in the front door.

"Not yet." The fire crackled cheerily, its reflection dancing on the rich green tiles and copper trim around the hearth.

There was the sound of a car stopping out front, car doors shutting and footsteps coming up the board walk and across the veranda. Wylie Clark went to open the door.

Introductions were made all around. John Wilson, the groom, in a Military Police uniform, looked nervous and pale as grooms often did. Jessie Patterson, the bride, a handsome young woman a good deal younger than her husband-to-be, looked shyly around the cozy room. Mrs. Patterson, the bride's mother, looked faintly disapproving; and James Patterson, Jessie's brother, took a quiet, smiling interest in the proceedings, the only person in the wedding party to look at ease.

But the Clarks were used to making people feel comfortable, nervous grooms and shy brides included, and the tension had eased before the little group gathered in front of the fireplace and the ceremony began. Mrs. Clark also stood as a witness.

At the lines "Till death us do part," Wilson gave his bride a particularly soulful look. His narrow hand trembled as he slipped a gold band on her finger.

"I now pronounce you man and wife," said the Reverend Clark with just as much feeling as if he'd been standing in the front of the large, imposing Knox Church, where he usually said these words. Conducting weddings was one of the nicest things about being a minister.

They didn't stay long after, only long enough to have a cup of tea and some of the dainties Mrs. Clark had thoughtfully provided. She hadn't had time to make sandwiches.

At the door, Wilson gripped the minister's hand as if he'd just given him a million dollars or saved him from some terrible fate. His hand was cold and damp.

"There's something to be said for getting married young," Wylie said to his wife as he helped clean up the tea things. "They're not so nervous when they're younger."

BOOK TWO

Sir, I Have the Honour to Report

Chapter XXII

✎ A FULL WEEK ✎

It was late on a Sunday night in October 1918, and Eileen Wismer had just finished preparing for Monday's meals. Lunch kits stood open and airing on the counter, a fresh loaf on the breadboard. Peas were shelled, potatoes scrubbed and ready for the pot, two tall jars packed with ginger snaps. The house was quiet. Eileen was almost always the last one up.

She'd missed Polly Wilson this week, and wondered how she was getting on in Saskatoon. She hoped he'd got a nice house for her. Eileen swept the floor, tapping the dustpan into the bin on the back porch, then closed the door and turned out the kitchen light. Part way down the dimly lit hall towards the stairs, she was startled by a knocking at the front door. John Wilson stood on the veranda, peering in the oval glass of the front door. She hurried to open it before he knocked again.

"Good evening, Mr. Wilson," she said. What was it they called him now? Inspector Wilson, was it?

"Good evening, Mrs. Wismer. I'm sorry to be around so late but I had business in Regina and have to leave again soon."

"Well, that's fine, I'm sure. I was still up." She looked hopefully past him. "Is Polly with you?"

"No." His expression was grave. Now that she'd turned the light on she saw how pale and edgy he looked.

"What?" she said. "What is it? Not bad news, I hope."

"Well, yes, it is, I'm sorry to say. We had a bad car accident, Polly and I."

"Oh, no!"

"Yes, at Saskatoon. And we had to walk four miles into Sutherland in the pouring rain. Polly is very ill, from being so wet and cold. She got hurt pretty bad in the accident, too."

"Well, I never! Oh, I'm so sorry to hear that, and just when she was going to get settled, with the baby coming and all. What—"

"I hate to hurry away, but I'm on business and just stopped in to see if there was any mail. It would cheer Polly up if she got some letters from home."

"Oh, yes, there is." Eileen hurried over to the rolltop desk in the parlour and came back with several envelopes—a large manila envelope for Wilson and three letters from Scotland for Polly. Wilson glanced at them and turned towards the door.

"Oh, just a minute, Mr. Wilson. I want to send Polly some cookies, ginger snaps are her favourite." Eileen hurried back to the kitchen and returned with a round blue tin rustling with cookies. "Tell her to keep the tin, and tell her I'll be praying for her to get well soon. Please let me know how she is."

"I will, Mrs. Wismer. Or Polly will. We'll just have to wait and see. Oh, Polly asked me to see if she'd left a black purse and gold brooch behind."

"Well, no," Eileen was surprised by the question. "Those were gifts from Mrs. Hansen. She had them with her in her bag when she left."

"Oh. I may have got her message wrong."

And he was gone again into the night.

Eileen Wismer was so rattled by Wilson's visit that she sat at the kitchen table in the dark for a long time, thinking: Why on earth didn't I ask what her injuries were? Why didn't he tell me? And if she was hurt so badly how could she walk four miles into Sutherland? And didn't Jack Wilson himself look like the wreck of the Hesperus? And that odd question about Polly's things. I doubt I'll get to sleep tonight for thinking about it.

❧

And, indeed, Wilson had had a week that might make anyone look like the wreck of the Hesperus. He'd been exhausted when he arrived at Blaine Lake, of course, and Jessie had taken one look at him and told him to go lie down. She had sounded none too pleased, since they'd planned to marry that day if possible, had actually thought they might marry the night before; he didn't know what he'd been thinking of to even consider that. And he'd have done it the Saturday no matter how he felt, but they couldn't get hold of a minister. Jessie hadn't arranged for one because she said he was always changing the plans.

Then on Sunday they'd got dressed up and gone with Jessie's mother and father to Marcelin, where there was a church service.

They'd timed their arrival for noon just as church let out. Jack went in to talk to the minister, a skinny sandy-haired pup not even dry behind the ears, who was busy packing up to get back to Saskatoon.

"Oh, I'm really sorry, sir, but I can't marry you. I'm not ordained yet."

Jack didn't like to remember the look on Jessie's face when he told her. His sweet Jessie, looking like a million dollars in her blue dress and hat and new red coat, leaning forward and smiling expectantly as he walked back to the car. When he told her, she looked as if she didn't know whether to scream or cry, but she looked none too fond of John Wilson at that moment.

"We'll just have to get married in Saskatoon," Jack said.

"I doubt very much if we'll ever get married at all," Jessie snapped. "That's all I've heard about for months on end and we're still not married."

"Now, now, Jessie," her father said.

Her mother sat staring straight ahead all the way back to Blaine Lake, just as mad as Jessie by the look of it.

"Jessie, we can surely find a minister in Saskatoon after church service tonight." Jack tried to take her hand, but she pulled it away, rummaging in her purse for the lace-edged handkerchief, "something borrowed" from her sister Kate.

"And how are we to get to Saskatoon, may I ask, since you've burned your car up? *My* car. I don't know why you had to take my car and wreck it."

"Calm down, Jessie," John Patterson said. "And don't forget, Jack's had an accident. He didn't do it on purpose. Jimmy can drive you to Saskatoon this afternoon if you want."

And that's what they did. And checked into the New Windsor Hotel after, just like any married couple, which was what they were. At last.

He needed a new car right away. The next morning he went to Riddell's Carriage Works and picked one out. He took Jessie back in the afternoon to take it for a drive. He was on pins and needles the whole time. Riddell didn't know he still owed money on the burned car, and he was worried about what Riddell's men might find at the culvert when they hauled the car in. And Riddell's secretary, Jean Brown, she'd made it worse, staring at him the whole time.

On Tuesday, the first of October, they moved out of the hotel and into the rooms he'd rented on 9th Street.

"You wouldn't be honeymooners now, would you?" the landlady had teased, showing them to the second-floor rooms. She had seen the wedding announcement in the paper that week. Jessie blushed and laughed, admitting they were, while all he could think of was, what if someone who knew Polly had seen the announcement? Jessie loved the rooms and they moved in the next day.

He'd also made two trips to the burned car that week, but by then he was beginning to settle down.

For Jessie it was a bit of a lark, being asked to go along with her husband and James Martin and Jim Matthews—policemen from Jack's office—as well as the two men from the garage, Mr. Southey and Walt Kelland.

The four of them drove out in the new car, with the men from the garage going in another car. She'd felt in a holiday mood: the day was beautiful, the fall colours glorious, and the car so lovely. Jack couldn't do enough for her. He was so touchingly _grateful_ to be married to her.

The world was suddenly full of possibilities. Jack said the way the war was going the Military Police would be disbanded soon, and the Mounties would be taking most of the men. They might even move to Vancouver, he said.

In the back seat, Martin and Matthews grinned at each other. Wilson spent so much time looking at his pretty young wife they were in danger of running in the ditch more than once. Well, maybe now he'd ease up on the booze, Martin thought.

When they got to the culvert, all of them got out to see the car. Martin walked right through the culvert, the earth a bit spongy with water seepage from the slough.

Southey and Kelland tried to pull the car out, but the front wheels were too bent.

"We'll have to come out later with the big truck and bring her in," Kelland said. "We'll just raise the front wheels up and tow her in on the back ones."

"Well," Jack said, "is everyone ready for dinner? My treat. Kind of a little wedding celebration."

And they all drove to a place about five miles away for the noon meal, with lots of lively talk and laughter among the six of them. Martin noticed that the boss had a couple of belts out behind the café, but it was a special occasion, after all. Jack Wilson looked more relaxed than they'd seen him for a long while.

❧

CANADIAN PACIFIC TELEGRAM CABLEGRAM
DEFERRED SERVICE
SASKATOON, SASK.
CANADA.
OCTOBER 15, 1918

WILLIAM HUTCHISON
CASTLEHILL
SLAMANNAN
STIRLINGSHIRE
SCOTLAND
POLLY AND I FOUND GOOD HOUSE. CAN YOU CABLE £100?
JACK

GREAT NORTH WESTERN TELEGRAPH COMPANY
PRINCE ALBERT, SASK.
OCTOBER 15, 1918

MRS. WISMORE
2039 ROSE STREET
REGINA, SASK.
PLEASE SEND TRUNKS TO CN EXPRESS OFFICE, PRINCE
ALBERT. WILL WRITE.
POLLY

Eileen Wismer wrote to Polly at Blaine Lake to ask how things were going and to say she was still looking for a letter. She wrote on the envelope, "To be opened by Mrs. Polly Wilson only." She was a bit surprised when, instead of a letter, she received another telegram:

GREAT NORTH WESTERN TELEGRAPH COMPANY
PRINCE ALBERT, SASK.
OCTOBER 25, 1918

MRS. WISMORE
2039 ROSE STREET
REGINA, SASK.
I DID NOT KNOW YOU WOULD BE WORRIED ABOUT ME. HAVE BEEN TRAVELLING ROUND WITH JACK FROM PLACE TO PLACE. WHEN SETTLED WILL WRITE.

POLLY

Chapter xxiii

PALE HORSE, PALE RIDER

Behold a pale horse: and his name that sat on him was Death.
—Revelation 6:8

Jack and Jessie Wilson were living at the house on 9th Street when the first cases of Spanish influenza broke out. Jack, weakened by stress and his bout with TB, was a made-to-order victim. The first cases appeared in Saskatoon on October 15, 1918, and spread like fire. Schools and theatres promptly closed, and infected houses were placarded. An emergency hospital was set up at Emmanuel College, and teachers at Victoria School operated a food kitchen. Before it was over, about 250 people from Saskatoon would die. In the town of Rosetown, not far from Saskatoon, the undertaker ran out of room in the morgue and took over the lumber yard to store bodies. The disease swept voraciously through Regina. In Moose Jaw, bodies piled up as terrified gravediggers refused to go to work. Winnipeg suffered 12,863 cases and 824 deaths. In The Pas, Manitoba, a carpenter built coffins in his kitchen. To help him keep up with the work, the priest would bring him measurements of those not yet dead. Columns of brief obituaries filled the newspapers, along with the "killed-in-action" announcements.

The Wilsons, fearful for Jack's weak lungs, went to visit Jessie's sister Kate, north of Prince Albert. There, just weeks after their wedding, Wilson fell ill with Spanish flu.

"Spanish" flu was a misnomer. China, France, the United States and Britain all experienced the deadly form of flu before it broke out in Spain in May 1918. But countries at war censored their press, and Spain, a neutral country, was the first to address it in a cable to London: "A strange form of disease of epidemic character has appeared in Madrid."

Influenza, so named because of the medieval belief that disease was influenced by the stars, was not new; the nineteenth century saw six major epidemics. Usually it affected the old and the very young, but this new strain was different; it attacked mostly those between twenty and forty years of age, a tragedy of catastrophic proportions to a world that had lost so many young men to war.

The worldwide epidemic, or pandemic, struck in the spring and the fall of 1918 and the early months of 1919. It's believed that American soldiers brought the disease to the trenches with them. In those cold, wet trenches of Germany, France and Belgium, chilled, underfed, exhausted soldiers on both sides succumbed by the thousands; in October 1919, 180,000 cases were reported in the German army. Guns on both sides fell silent. The previous May, the British fleet, with over 10,000 sailors sick, was unable to leave port. They had multitudes for company, among them King George V and Franklin Delano Roosevelt, the thirty-six-year-old assistant secretary of the American navy. The imperial chancellor of Germany was also ill. It seems likely that Spanish flu shortened the war.

When it was over, thousands headed for home incubating the germ—many men survived the horrors of war only to be struck down by Spanish flu. Fatalities on troopships were twice that on land, and many on their way home were buried at sea, as were many on their way to the front. The flu arrived in eastern Canada by one such troopship. Returned men fanned out on trains across Canada, sometimes carried off before their destination. And so it spread. And spread. Nothing in human history—no war and no other plague—killed so many so quickly. Worldwide, more than twenty million died.

Onset was often stunningly swift, and in the last stages—sometimes only hours after the first—it resembled the Black Death in that the patient's skin often took on a dark-blue or black hue. Those who vomited up copious quantities of blood seemed to recover faster, though often fifty or sixty pounds lighter and with a lifetime legacy of heart and respiratory problems.

It attacked Wilson first, Jessie soon after. Somehow they made their way to the Pattersons in Blaine Lake, who, if the newspaper accounts were right, were not likely to catch it. Once again his very survival depended on the Patterson family, who could be forgiven if they secretly wished they'd never laid eyes on him.

"Dangerous age 26–30," headlined the Regina *Leader*. Not so in the Patterson house; in attempting to look after Jessie and Jack, Allison and John immediately came down with it and were seriously ill themselves.

Most people quietly did what they could for their stricken neighbours, though it was often a terrible dilemma whether to help sick neighbours at the risk of infecting your own family. The flu was capricious, to say the least, sometimes killing an entire family, or randomly choosing one or two. The Swiss called it the Coquette for its fickle nature and its propensity to pass its favours around so freely.

In the Patterson household, all survived, and the future looked bright. Peace was just over the horizon.

When the Armistice was signed on the eleventh hour of the eleventh day of the eleventh month, celebrations erupted. Bonfires burned in Trafalgar Square, and Saskatchewan farmers lit up the sky with burning straw stacks. Hoarded bottles suddenly appeared as Kaiser Wilhelm crackled in effigy. And many of those who were sick felt their hearts lighten. The war was over, and the flu, or the worst of it, had passed. For many it was a joyful time, for others one of acute sadness.

As Katherine Anne Porter wrote at the end of her story "Pale Horse, Pale Rider," "No more war, no more plague, only the dazed silence that follows the ceasing of heavy guns; noiseless houses with the shades drawn, empty streets, the dead cold light of tomorrow. Now there would be time for everything."

Chapter XXIV

✒ I HAVE NOT BEEN GOOD IN MY TIME ✒

Jack Wilson would say later that during this period, shortly after his marriage to Jessie and his bout with the flu, his mind was "all to pieces." In a little more than a year he had fallen madly in love, suffered a serious case of TB, lost his job, and his wife had arrived out of the blue. Then he had started an important new job, committed a murder, got married again, nearly died of Spanish flu, and moved four times.

The following letter from a man he worked with in Saskatoon, with its reminder "now don't forget this," seems to substantiate his claim. It also supports a later report that he was playing fast and loose with the Military Service Act fines he collected.

> CMPC
> Alexandra School,
> November 21, 1918.

Dear Jack:

Your Chief Reid came after me today in Regina in regard to the trip we had in Birch Hills and he showed me the case of Alf Schmitz. Now I gave him a list of all the men who were fined and the costs. All and every case, I made the costs $3.50. Now don't forget this, as they are still looking for some loophole. Alf Schmitz's costs were somewhere about $45.00 or $50.00, but don't forget the costs were only $3.50 in all cases.

Now I don't know what to say to you only I still have possession of your rifle and could not see anyone who I could trust to give it you on my way through.

I hope you and your Mrs. are in the enjoyment of good health as I am at present. So now bye-bye.

> I beg to remain,
> your sincere friend,
> W. H. Stoddart

The extra money Wilson pocketed more than likely helped him to finance his double life, including the purchase of the car for Jessie.

✒

In Scotland, Polly's family were by now very concerned. Her parents and her sister Nellie tried to hide it from the children, but they conferred often with other family members by letter and on visits. The silence from across the ocean became louder by the day. Helen Hutchison read and reread Polly's last letter, dated September 15.

"Over two whole months now, Nellie. And Polly knows how the children love Christmas."

"It is strange, Mother, I can't deny it. And Lizzie's still not received the letter Polly said she'd write as soon as she got settled in Saskatoon."

"Now, now. Let's not borrow trouble." William Hutchison didn't believe in borrowing anything. "We'll hear something soon."

And they did. Or at least Elizabeth's husband, Archie, did.

> Box 287,
> Sutherland, Saskatchewan.
> 14th December, 1918
>
> Dear Archie,
>
> I am writing this to tell you what awful trouble Polly and I have had since the Spanish Influenza broke out. I was transferred to Saskatoon about the middle of October to take charge of the Northern half of the Province and the salary was increased to $200.00 per month and $6.00 per day expenses. Polly and I was so pleased about it. Influenza broke out at the same time and owing to Polly's condition and so many deaths amongst women in that state that we were afraid. A Doctor advised me to take her away out in the country up North and try and evade the flu. We went in my Police car and I got laid up and I got up too soon. Then took a relapse and took pneumonia. Before getting delirious I told the Doctor to spare no expense with Polly so he got two trained nurses for day and night duty. We were both very ill.
>
> I got out a week ago for the first time as one of the nurses wanted to quit. I had to go all the way to Regina to get another one they are so hard to get. Then I got sick on the way home and was laid up again until yesterday. Neither one of us was expected to live but although Polly is very weak the Doctor says there is no danger now if she is only careful and she has not to get up for at least two weeks yet. For myself I am a wreck now. I

only weigh 132 pounds and my lung is very bad again. I don't know what it is to get a good sleep. As soon as I go to bed I start coughing. I have seen a lung specialist and he told me frankly that I will not live many months. Now, Archie, as soon as Polly is strong enough to travel I will tell her and we will come home. I want to see the children before the end.

It is hard, Archie, I have not been good in my day and then I was making such good money that soon we would have been well fixed. I had a good job and a big responsibility but I could handle it. It is very hard. My pay is still going on yet but likely it will be stopped soon unless I get strong enough to work until Polly is well enough.

You can tell Father and Mother, Archie, that I spared no expense on Polly since she got laid up. I am paying one nurse $30.00 and the other $25.00 per week and I have already paid the Doctor $300.00.

But, Archie, I had to save Polly. I knew if I took the flu that the old lung trouble would come back and likely finish me. I got Jim's letter and meant to reply to it but got laid up a few days after I received it.

Polly did not lose the baby and the Doctor says everything will be alright provided she is careful. I will bring her home as soon as she is strong enough and, Archie, I am going to leave it to you to pay her just what you think the firm owes me but we can settle all that when we come home.

Now I am going to close now as my arm is getting shaky writing.

The deaths from the flu here have been very high. Up in the North they are finding homesteaders dead in their shacks everywhere. I will write Father and Mother in a few days again.

> Your loving brother,
> John

Archie Craig bundled up in warm clothes, wheeled out his bicycle, and rode through the blustery cold rain the twenty-three miles to Slamannan to break the awful news to Polly's parents.

In Regina, Mrs. Wismer received a letter written the same day.

> Box 287
> Sutherland, Sask.
> 14th Decr. 1918

Mrs. Wismore

Dear Madam,

I have been asked by Polly to write and tell you our troubles for the past 10 weeks; when I left you the last time I came back to Saskatoon the same night and felt sick. I went to the doctor and he advised me to get out in the country and try and keep away from the influenza owing to the conditon of my lungs. Telling him about Mrs. Wilson and her condition and what we expected early in the year he said she must try and keep away from the flu if possible. We started out in the country and I got laid up with flu in a few days then took pneumonia then Polly took ill. I got out for the first time a week ago yesterday. Polly is very ill yet but is now out of danger. It was very hard that we took ill in the country but maybe it was for the best.

As soon as Polly took ill the doctor advised me to get a trained nurse for her as he was afraid it would be hard on her owing to her condition. We got 2 Nurses for her, one for night duty, and thanks to the Doctor she is now out of danger but so weak that they only allow me to go in for a short time daily. I cabled home a few days ago for her and got a reply that none of them at home are sick.

As for myself I was down at Fort Qu'Appelle Sanatorium on Thursday being examined and the doctor says my lung is so bad now that he does not think I will live till the Spring. I only weigh 132 lbs and can only walk about 3 blocks without a rest. As soon as Polly gets well enough to move I am going to bring her to Regina for a little while then I shall have to tell her what the doctor says about me and we shall go home if I am strong enough as I want to see the children. It is very hard. I have not been very good in my time but I am thankful I have been able to spare no expense in Polly's illness so that she will be able to look after the children. I came down here today from Prince Albert in connection with my work. I want to try and hold my job for a little while yet as the wages are good and Polly will need all the money I can get for her before I get laid up again. I don't know what it is to get a good sleep, I cough all night long. I am going back to Polly tonight again.

I want to ask a favour from you, Mrs. Wismore; will you try and give Polly a room and look after her as soon as she is well enough to stand the trip. For myself, I will not ask you to take me as consumption is so infectious . . . but as soon as she is strong enough she would like to come down beside you until she is strong enough to make the trip home.

It is very hard all this trouble coming on us but we are not so bad as some. There has been so many deaths with the influenza that we ought to be thankful.

Your sincere friend,

John Wilson

P.S. In your reply please address it to Box 287 Sutherland as I am staying with our friends there while I am in Saskatoon and I shall have to come down next week again.

J. Wilson

That same night, after the house was quiet, Eileen Wismer brought writing paper, pen and ink into the warm kitchen. It would be a difficult, but she had to answer Jack Wilson's letter. This awful flu. That poor man. She didn't like him, but he seemed to be sorry now, what did he say? That he had not been good in his day? At least he admitted it. And you had to pity a man in his condition, no matter what you felt about him personally, and do what you could to ease his burden. She would talk to him of religious matters. Everyone had to face up to it in the end.

Eileen dipped the pen and began to write.

∽

The Canadian National Railway express office in Prince Albert was crowded, as always, with trunks, boxes and parcels of every description, and Ned Storie had to lean over the two trunks for the umpteenth time to reach something on a higher shelf. As if this job wasn't hard enough on the back without people using the place as a storage depot.

"Have we heard anything yet about these two trunks from Regina?" he called testily to someone in the adjoining office.

"No." His assistant came to the door. "Do you want me to write a letter to that Mrs. Wismer?"

"Yes, damn it. I've just tripped over the blasted things for the forty-seventh time. Ask her if we can send them back there or what?"

"All right, Mr. Storie. I'll do it after the next train."

"Damned funny," Storie said. "They've been here two months, just

103

about. Tell her to send us Mrs. Wilson's address. Maybe there's some mixup and she doesn't know they're here."

"Yes, sir, I'll do that." And he bounded off at the urgent clicking of the telegraph.

Ned Storie rolled his eyes behind his assistant's back. Eager young pup. He hated being called sir.

There was no reply from Mrs. Wismer, but about a month later, a postcard arrived from Mrs. Wilson herself: "Sick with flu in the Sutherland Hospital. Please hold trunks till I can call for them. Please advise me at Box 287, Sutherland, as to charges against them. Mrs. Polly Wilson."

A postal notice was sent to Mrs. Wilson at that address notifying her of the charges against the shipments, and the postcard was pinned to the On Hand card in the office. Eventually the trunks were moved into the back of the storage shed, since it looked as if Mrs. Wilson, poor soul, had not survived the flu.

Shortly after, Ned Storie moved to Edmonton as express agent for the Great Northern Railway. It would be another year before anyone showed the slightest interest in Polly Wilson's trunks.

❧

When the first payment for Wilson's new car was conspicuous by its absence, Mr. Riddell was none too pleased. He'd allowed Wilson two hundred dollars for the old burned car, but when he saw it he knew he'd been cheated. He was lucky to get a few spare parts from it.

"Well, I've learned my lesson. A policeman's uniform doesn't guarantee anything," he told his friends.

Riddell was just hurrying back to the garage after his morning tea one frigid December day when he saw John Wilson across the street.

"Wilson! Wilson!"

Wilson stopped, and Riddell hurried over.

"Could I talk to you a minute, please? You know your car payment didn't come through." Now he was closer, Riddell saw that Wilson looked pale and thin as a rake.

"Yes, I know, I was coming to see you about it. I've been very ill with flu and now I've got TB." Riddell stepped back a bit. "I just came from the sanatorium at Fort Qu'Appelle and I have to go back for a year."

"Oh, is that so?" Why didn't he believe the man? For one thing he didn't think people with TB were allowed to come and go from the sanatorium as if it was a hotel, and go roaming around the country giving it to other people. If they could, no wonder there was so much of it around.

"I'm expecting some money from the old country any day now and will make sure you get paid," Wilson said.

Riddell phoned the doctor at the Fort Qu'Appelle Sanatorium next day and was told they'd never heard of John Wilson.

Around Christmas time he saw Wilson again and asked about the money.

"I was just going to cable Scotland for the money to pay you."

"Good. I'll go with you right now."

And he did, standing at Wilson's elbow while he sent the cable.

"That's good, then. I'll see you in a day or two, Wilson."

As soon as Riddell turned the corner, Jack went back in and cancelled the cable.

The car dealer had yet to learn that the burned car he'd purchased for two hundred dollars had a three-hundred-dollar lien against it in favour of J. A. Erskine, the Grey Dort agent in Regina. Eventually Riddell would repossess the new car—"in rotten condition"—and judge himself out about six hundred dollars from his dealings with Inspector Wilson.

❧

Wilson was still drinking heavily. In early January, on a train trip to Blaine Lake with Jessie, they bumped into Sergeant Drysdale, whom Wilson knew from the Prince Albert Mounted Police detachment.

"I want you to meet my wife, Jessie. We got married last fall."

Sergeant Drysdale was on his way to Prince Albert, and they sat together till the Wilsons got off at Blaine Lake.

"I'll soon be back in the service myself," Jack said. Drysdale could smell liquor on him. Wilson got up and lurched off to the washroom, laughing and trying to pretend the movement of the train had thrown him off balance.

Jessie looked embarrassed.

Chapter xxv

⟶ WAITING ⟵

Another Hogmanay, a year since Polly's announcement that she was going to look for Jack. The family gathered and compared notes, even though there were no new notes to compare. It was now more than three months since Polly had written, and they grew more anxious by the day.

"I wrote and sent the three newspapers in September, and told Polly that Lizzie was wondering if they'd received the hundred pounds," Helen said. "Polly wrote right back and said she'd write to Lizzie in a few days, as soon as she got settled in Saskatoon."

"And I never heard a word," Elizabeth said, though they all knew it. They had gone over and over it.

They kept their voices low. The children were in bed; they hadn't even asked to stay up for First Foot.

"Well, don't forget there was that letter from Jack in December," James said, "about the flu. And how much money he spent on doctors and nurses," he added, with a trace of sarcasm.

"I know," Helen Hutchison said. "But that was from Jack, and so much later. Why wouldn't Polly write a word to us after she moved to Saskatoon? Before she fell ill?"

William Hutchison turned from putting more coal on the fire. "Well, don't forget, Mother, it seems long but it's only a bit over three months. There'll be a lot of extra mail with the war ending, and Christmas and all. And before that she was down with flu."

"Maybe after all that's happened she'd be embarrassed to say if she and Jack aren't getting on," Nellie said.

But Polly's mother would not be comforted. She shook her head, her lips tight. "That would never stop Polly writing. Especially to the children. Even just a postcard."

Then, finally, twelve days later, news arrived in the form of a cable-gram: "OUT TODAY FOR THE FIRST TIME. JACK AGAIN SICK. BOTH COMING HOME NEXT MONTH. POLLY."

"Polly never sent us that," said her mother. And no one could convince her otherwise.

If Helen Hutchison's skepticism rubbed off on the rest of the family, the second cable, addressed to Archie, dispelled it completely. "BOTH LEAVING FOR HOME NEXT WEEK VIA PANAMA CANAL. CAN YOU SEND £100. JOHN."

No one in the world would be so cruel as to send such a message to an anxious family if it wasn't so. Especially to the children, that was unimaginable.

The preparations for the glad reunion began; the cooking and baking, the cleaning and polishing of Polly's and Jack's house, the sewing of new clothes for the young ones to go to meet their parents, presents lovingly made by the bairns. And the children got more excited with each passing day.

And then they waited.

And waited . . .

∾

Foreseeing a period of unrest after the war, in December 1918, the Canadian government issued an order that the RNWMP be recruited from 303 men to a strength of 1,200. They also recalled the detachments serving in France and Siberia.

With the war over, the need to enforce the Military Service Act was over, and the Civil Section of the Military Police was disbanded. Men serving in that force were, for the most part, absorbed into the RNWMP. Wilson got his wish to be back in the Mounties.

On January 6, when he was re-engaged, he gave his next of kin as Mary (Polly) Wilson, 217 9th Street, Saskatoon. He spent three weeks at Regina headquarters, then his first posting came through. On January 21, Jack and Jessie left for Blairmore, Alberta, in the Crow's Nest Pass.

They left a trunk and some boxes, including Wilson's shotgun, in a shed at Con Read's place. In late February, Jack Wilson was granted a request to be transferred to Vancouver. There were now a thousand miles and a mountain range between him and that shallow grave near Waldheim.

∾

One cold January day, Mrs. Laing, the Hutchisons' old friend from Slamannan, and Eileen Wismer were conferring over tea in the Wismers' parlour. A fire crackled in the hearth and the good smell of roasting chicken wafted out from the kitchen.

"I was so hoping you'd have some good news I could take back to Scotland."

"I wish I had some for you, but I haven't had a word from her in her own hand, only that telegram. And I know she'd have written if she was all right."

"You don't think it's just that things aren't—you know." They both knew about the other woman.

"No. She'd have let me know when the baby was born. I know she would." She counted on her fingers. "You see, that baby would be here by now; it was her third so it wouldn't be late, not likely."

"Unless she lost the baby because of that car accident."

"If there *was* a car accident. Policeman or no policeman, I don't trust Jack Wilson. I never did."

"Oh, dear. I just don't know what to think. Do you?"

"Well, something is seriously wrong. And with him in the police force he can say what he wants and people will believe him."

They paused for a moment, as if both considering what they might really be saying.

"And Polly such a sweet girl, she always was."

"Yes, as nice as they come. I feel sorry for you having to talk to her folks in Scotland, Mrs. Laing."

Mrs. Laing sighed and shook her head. Yes, indeed.

~

"He *what*?" Helen Hutchison cried, then covered her mouth with her hand. She didn't want to waken Father.

"That's what he told me on the phone," Mrs. Laing said. "After I went to see Mrs. Wismer, I phoned the police headquarters in Regina, and Jack himself answered the phone."

"And he said Polly was in an accident? We never heard that. Was she hurt badly?"

"He said she was nearly killed, but was recovered now."

"Nearly killed? He told us she only had a bad case of flu."

Helen Hutchison looked as if she might faint, and Mrs. Laing quickly got her a glass of water, which she drank, spilling a bit on her blue afternoon dress. It was almost dark in the parlour. A cold, steady rain streamed down the windows.

"He told me she had just a trifling case of flu, but that it was a very bad accident."

"Oh, I just don't understand it!" Helen wailed. "Something is far wrong, I know it, though they all keep saying I mustn't think that way. And William's heart attack, that was nothing in the world but worrying himself over our poor girl."

Helen herself looked frail. She'd aged a great deal since her friend saw her last.

"I'm so sorry. I thought maybe it was good news, about her being recovered from the accident."

"Oh no, you mustn't feel bad, Mrs. Laing. We appreciate all you've done. We've tried everything to get news, but it's all so far away, isn't it? If only she'd never gone. It's all I think of."

Chapter XXVI

∽ VANCOUVER ∾

Jack and Jessie delighted in Vancouver and spent many happy hours taking in the sights of that burgeoning city on the west coast. Soon Jack's old pal Conrad Read, who had also joined the force, would be there. Jack had pulled some strings to get Con posted to Vancouver. Nell, Con's wife, would be company for Jessie, too. Jack was doing good work and now had three stripes on his sleeve. He had, not surprisingly, displayed a flair for undercover assignments. What's more, the mild coastal climate, more like the old country, agreed with him, and he was gaining weight.

Life was good once again—if he didn't think too much. But there were always reminders. As in Con's last letter:

By the way, I have your gun. I did not take it to a gunsmith, but cleaned it myself, in fact am still at it. It was in pretty bad shape, but is coming round now. I got back to Saskatoon the morning after you left and I was mad that I had missed you. Saskatoon is about the same. We had two weeks of pretty cold weather but now the streets are almost clear of snow and the autos are appearing in force.

That cold Saskatchewan world—and everything connected with it—was thankfully far away. They hadn't seen snow since they left, and Jessie'd been like a wide-eyed child on the trip out. He'd spent an awful lot of money, wanting to give her the best of everything, and he didn't regret it.

And to a small town prairie girl like Jessie, Vancouver was astonishing, the height of elegance with its Victorian towers, turrets and gingerbread work, its thick lawns and monkey puzzle trees. Men in bowler hats and Chinese houseboys jostled elbows on the streets, women in handsome driving habits and traps trotted thoroughbreds around Stanley Park, and weekend holidayers crowded the huge pier and beach at English Bay. Traffic drove on the left side of the streets, in the British style. And Jessie was too timid to drive. New buildings were springing up all over. And everywhere there was the exhilarating smell of the ocean and the excited cries of gulls. It was a far cry from Blaine Lake.

But all was not idyllic. Jack was doing undercover work now. He was away a lot and still drinking too much, often in the line of duty, he said, with suspects, mostly dockworkers, but still . . . And his moods were unpredictable when he drank, sometimes frighteningly black. She had hidden his service revolver more than once when he threatened to kill himself. He hadn't done that lately, but he still woke pale and sweating from terrible nightmares. It was all very upsetting. And Jessie missed her family, especially her mother.

Jack still hadn't produced the divorce papers Jessie so needed to see. Both his sisters were dead, he had told her, but his brother Alex must be home again. Why couldn't he send the papers? Or Jack's lawyer? Or the Reverend Haxworthy—was that his name?—who was so close to the Wilson family? (Actually, the good reverend's name was Hampwell.) Surely there was someone. She didn't understand it, and couldn't help but wonder sometimes if she was legally married.

On April 15, the Reads arrived, and Conrad Read handed Jack Wilson his shotgun.

∽

The day before, in Wilson's home village in Scotland, Elizabeth Craig sat down to write a letter.

Tinto View
Kilncadzow
Carluke, Scotland
14.4.19

Mr. Routledge, Superintendant,
Royal North West Mounted Police,
Prince Albert, Sask.

Dear Sir:

Owing to your past kindness I again take the liberty of making use of same. As you know, my sister came out to Canada to her husband Mr. John Wilson (as it was in your office she found him) in April of last year (1918).

We had letters from her every mail up till end of September when Mr. Wilson got promotion under Dominion [Military] Police and was sent to Saskatoon. Since going there we have never received a letter from my sister.

Wilson wrote my husband on 14th December saying he had been dangerously ill with the "flu" and that my sister was expected to get better but was not out of danger but that he had not many months to live and that as soon as his wife was able to travel he would bring her home to Father and Mother as he wanted to see his children before the end.

Mr. Routledge, you can understand how we all felt on receiving this letter and my husband went home to Slamannan to break the awful news to my poor father and mother.

About the middle of January, Father received a cable saying they were both much better and were sailing for Scotland the following month (February). The next week my husband received a cable saying he (Wilson) and Polly were sailing next week and would my husband cable

£100, that was the second £100. Since then we have received no news of them and naturally we looked and looked and waited till we began to worry very much about them both. Then my father had a bad heart attack (he is an old man now) and I went to see him and found out that he and mother were killing themselves with worry about their girl. So when I left I promised to get news for them soon. My husband met me with trap at station and when I told him how Father and Mother were worrying he cabled to Wilson to see if they were well and telling them of Father's illness; that was a fortnight past yesterday and no answer has as yet been received.

My husband went on Saturday to see Father and Mother and a Mrs. Laing has come from Regina who informs us that while my sister had the "flu" it was only trifling and that she had been nearly killed in a motor accident.

Now, Sir, can you understand any man saying his wife was dangerously ill with the flu when it was an accident? This wrong information combined with no answer to our cable and knowing the treatment Wilson meted out to my sister from the time he entered the M. Police has shattered all confidence we ever had in him and has greatly increased my father and mother's anxiety for their daughter. They entreated my husband to ask me to write to the gentleman who had been so kind before in making enquiries for my sister's husband so he promised I would be sure to do so.

Would you be so kind, Mr. Routledge, to enquire or cause enquiries to be made in Saskatoon for my sister and could you get the information from another source than Wilson as we would have no faith now in anything he told us about my sister—he was always a plausible liar (excuse my language but it exactly fits him). My husband bids me say he will be only too pleased to pay any expenses caused in finding out my sister. We never had their Saskatoon address but he is in Saskatoon with Dominion Police.

We would give anything to have definite news of her. The uncertainty is keeping my father (who is the best father in the world to his children) from recovering and indeed my hubby says it is killing him.

Oh, Sir, will you do your best to relieve an old man and woman's anxiety about their child? My father has got it into his head that my sister is dead—perhaps foul play—and you know once old people get a notion into their mind it is not easy to remove it.

Will you please write by return or as soon as you get any news for us (don't rely on what Wilson says) as we will anxiously await your reply.

Thanking you for your past trouble and kindness for us and in anticipation of another to us,

> I remain,
> Dear Sir,
> Yours v. gratefully,
> Elizabeth Craig

When Elizabeth refers to Routledge's "past kindness" she is referring to letters he wrote in reply to queries about Wilson's whereabouts before Polly came over. This outstanding police officer would start the ball rolling in the investigation into Polly's disappearance.

Chapter XXVII

∽ SPRING ∾

Spring has come to the prairies; the snow is melted, the sloughs full, the duns and browns and ochres of early spring veiled in a soft haze of green. By the culvert near Waldheim, robins swoop from tree to tree with twigs: derisive crows trade insults between fence posts; a meadowlark at the edge of the field pauses in its labours to throw back its head and fling a joyous song over and over into the soft blue sky. Ducks skim the ponds. Bees investigate the first flowers, and under the greening grasses and ground cover all manner of insects go about their industrious insect lives. Mauve and purple crocuses, their petals cupped in downy silver-grey sepals, have sprouted overnight. Singly and in clumps they bask among sea-green sage and prairie grass. Plain, sturdy, honest little flowers. A lot like Polly Wilson, who knows nothing of this spring, nor ever will of another.

Chapter xxviii

⌁ SOMETHING FISHY ⌁

On May 10, Assistant Commissioner Routledge wrote a letter that would open the investigation into Polly Wilson's disappearance. In a letter to Superintendent Fitzpatrick Joseph Horrigan at the Vancouver detachment, he asked Horrigan to ascertain from Regimental Number 6020 (Wilson's number) the present whereabouts and address of his wife. Routledge had received inquiries from the old country and would be happy to have this information without delay.

F. J. Horrigan promptly replied that Number 6020's wife was living with him in Vancouver.

On May 16, Routledge wrote to Polly's sister:

Mrs. Elizabeth Craig,

Tinto View, Kilncadzow,

Carluke, Scotland.

Dear Madam:

I am in receipt of your letter of the 14th ultimo making inquiries as to the whereabouts of the wife of Corporal [sic] John Wilson of the RNWM Police and in reply would say that Mrs. Wilson is at present living with her husband.

If you wish to communicate with her, I would advise sending your letter, under cover, addressed to Superintendent F. J. Horrigan, RNWM Police, 706 Credit Foncier Building, Vancouver, B.C.

Yours very truly,

W. H. Routledge

Assistant Commissioner

Elizabeth was euphoric! At last, after seven and a half months, news of Polly from a reliable source! She was in Vancouver, which must mean she had recovered from the flu or the accident or both. It meant she was alive, anyway.

What wonderful news to send home to her parents! Archie again set off for Slamannan on his bicycle to tell the Hutchisons, but they received the news with skepticism and did not write themselves.

Elizabeth wrote a long, joyous letter to Polly, enclosing it in a letter to Superintendent Horrigan. Because she couldn't get rid of a niggling doubt herself, she included a picture of Polly in her letter to Horrigan. She didn't have a recent picture, so she sent the photo she'd had taken with the children. The picture of Polly, so sober except for the tiny smile pulling at the corner of her mouth, made Elizabeth smile. Now they would hear from Polly with an explanation for her long silence. There had to be a reason.

∽

In a force known for men dedicated to their work, Fitzpatrick Joseph Horrigan was known as an exceptionally hard worker. In 1918, when he asked for two months' leave to visit family in Ontario, he noted in a letter to Commissioner Perry that in all his years of service (nineteen years to that time) he had taken only ten days off. He never married. He was fifty-eight years old the summer of 1919, a strict but just officer and, in private life, a genial and warm-hearted man.

Superintendent Horrigan read the letter from Elizabeth and looked with interest at the picture of Polly and the children. He hadn't realized that Wilson had any children. He got up and opened his office door. Sergeant James Cather was gazing out the window by his desk at the sparkling spring day.

"Come into my office a minute, Sergeant. If you aren't too busy."

Sergeant Cather smiled. "Of course, sir." The superintendent had his testy moments, but his staff sergeant put them down to his failing health and took no offence.

In his office, Horrigan handed him the letter addressed to Polly Wilson.

"Will you see that Sergeant Wilson gets this mail from Scotland? His wife's family seem to be quite anxious about Mrs. Wilson."

Sergeant Cather looked with curiosity at the photograph on Horrigan's desk.

"That's Wilson's wife, apparently. I didn't know he had children, did you?" Horrigan slid the photo across the desk.

"No, I had no idea." He looked closely at the picture of Polly and the children.

"Close-mouthed chap. Good thing, I guess, for a secret agent."

"Yes, I would say so, sir. I'll arrange to meet him somewhere other than his house as soon as possible."

"Yes, that's right. We can't break his cover. Tell him I said to get in touch with the family without delay. I'm sure it's just an oversight. The sister-in-law sounds like the worrying kind."

"Yes, sir. I'll take care of it."

And he would, too. Horrigan was seriously ill and would soon have to ask for a leave of absence. James Cather, his staff sergeant, did everything he could to ease his workload. In an August 1919, letter to the commissioner, Horrigan described Cather as "smart, striking, courteous, and gentlemanly," and commented on his "strong character and strict probity." He must have been very striking indeed; a blue-eyed, black-haired Irishman, well over six feet tall, and thirty-four years old that summer of 1919. Superintendent Horrigan went on to say, "In looking over the past six months I really often wonder how I could have got along without his valuable assistance."

Sergeant Cather had talents even Superintendent Horrigan wasn't aware of. He had at one time worked in a bank, which he subsequently robbed.

∾

On a soft July evening, Sergeant Cather set out for his usual brisk walk after supper. He turned towards English Bay, where the sun winked in every tiny wave, and the bracing air filled his lungs. He loved this walk along the sea to Stanley Park.

And there, around a bend, walking just ahead were a slim man in plainclothes with a familiar back and walk and a willowy woman holding his arm. Sergeant Jack Wilson. Sergeant Cather hurried to catch up, and a flustered-looking Wilson introduced him to Mrs. Wilson.

A few weeks ago Sergeant Cather had met Wilson in an out-of-the-way café to deliver the mail from Scotland, including the photograph and the directive from Horrigan to get in touch with the family. Wilson said he couldn't understand why their cable and letters hadn't been received but he promised to take care of it immediately.

Now Sergeant Cather smiled and took the hand of the slim young woman with sculptured cheekbones. This was definitely not the woman in the photograph.

"How do you do, Sergeant," she said.

"And how are you enjoying Vancouver, Mrs. Wilson?" he asked.

"Oh, it's lovely, isn't it? Now that it's stopped raining."

"Yes, it is indeed. Well, I must get on and leave you to your walk," he said, and strode on ahead like any man out for a serious constitutional. Since Wilson was undercover he mustn't linger anyway, nor would it do to about face and hurry straight back to report to Horrigan.

Probably an oversight, Horrigan had said, but this was a different woman altogether, and she didn't look old enough to have two chidren. Some oversight, Sergeant Cather thought. When he turned around and walked back the way he'd come, there was no sign of Jack Wilson and the woman he called his wife. The shoreline here smelled fishy. It was not the only thing.

∼

Constable Brickton, Wilson's liaison with the office, was often at the Wilson's house on Homer Street that summer. During the first week of July, he and Wilson were sitting on the veranda talking, when Wilson went into the kitchen to get a drink. As he started back, he heard Brickton talking to Jessie in the living room.

"Oh, Mrs. Wilson, I must tell you, a strange thing happened in the office today."

"Oh?" said Jessie. "What was that?"

"Sergeant Cather showed me a photograph of a strange woman and asked me if that was Sergeant Wilson's wife." Brickton laughed.

Wilson's heart stopped beating momentarily.

"Really?" Jessie said.

"Yes. And she didn't look anything like you. I don't know where he got that idea."

Wilson drained his glass in a few swallows. When he'd steadied himself and walked back to the veranda, Jessie had gone upstairs. Nothing was ever mentioned about it.

Jessie had been wanting to go home to see her mother, and Jack now encouraged her to go. It would give him some time to think what he should do. Before she left, he took three days off work. He spent every moment with Jessie, his darling wee girl. Over and over he asked himself if he should take Jessie and run; she would go with him, he knew that. Then he put her on a train to Blaine Lake.

On July 31, Superintendent Horrigan wrote to Commissioner Perry with his concerns aroused by Elizabeth's letter and Sergeant Cather's report after meeting Jessie:

> This aroused my suspicion and I intended to take the matter up with you during your visit here, but it slipped my memory. While I cannot think that anything serious is the matter, still an investigation is unquestionably necessary. The photograph was that of a middle-aged person with 2 children, whereas the person at present living with Sgt. Wilson is quite young and it is understood that they have only been married a short time.
>
> I have not approached Sgt. Wilson on the subject, nor shall I do so until I hear from you. It would be most unfortunate if anything should be wrong, as he is the most important witness in our cases against the Russians now being held before the Immigration Board.

In the margin of the letter he wrote: "Sister states Mrs. Wilson 30 years of age."

❧

While Jessie was away, Wilson got out the dispatch case he'd used in the Military Police, the one Polly's body had fallen over and adhered to that terrible night by the culvert. Sitting at the kitchen table on Homer Street, he went through everything in it. He read his and Jessie's love letters once again, then looked through the other papers and returned them all, placing the dispatch case once again in the top of the trunk.

Conrad Read, visiting Jack at the house while Jessie was away, had occasion to look in Wilson's desk for something. In the bottom drawer lay a Colt .38 pistol. Read recognized it as one that had gone missing from the Saskatoon office a year ago. Thinking he must be mistaken, he looked at it closely, but the butt was chipped in exactly the same place. It was strange Jack never told him he had the gun. He sat at the desk for a while, thinking about it. There'd been such a commotion in the office about it, all the men questioned one by one, suspicion cast on Corporal DeBoard, who Wilson said had had the gun last. Conrad felt vaguely insulted now. He should ask Jack what the devil was going on, but, like Jessie, he said nothing. .

Wilson, expecting to be called in for questioning any day, perhaps even detained, tried to talk Jessie into staying longer in Blaine Lake. She stayed one extra week, and on August 15, she stepped off the train into her husband's waiting arms. Then the weeks stretched on with no more word of inquiries, a reprieve Wilson put down to the fact that Superintendent Horrigan had been ill in hospital for some time. Polly's family would not give up. He knew that now. Especially Elizabeth.

Chapter xxix
✍ ANNIVERSARY ❧

In late September, on the anniversary of their last letter from Polly herself, the family renewed their efforts to get some word of her. William Hutchison couldn't rest, and no one could make him. He paced and fretted his way through the days.

On September 18, Nellie Hutchison wrote to Mrs. Wismer, asking if there was something she could tell the family about Polly that she had not told Mrs. Laing. And Elizabeth again took up her pen.

> Tinto View
> Kilncadzow
> Carluke, Lanarkshire
> Scotland.
> 23-9-1919

Superintendent Horrigan
Dear Sir:
I wrote you on 3rd June enclosing a letter addressed to Mrs. Jno. Wilson . . . but up to the present time I have not received an answer from you . . . We had such hopes on getting Mr. Routledge's letter, that

they were living in Vancouver . . . but hope deferred makes the heart sick. It is now 8 months since we received John Wilson's cable saying he and his wife (my sister) were leaving for home via the Panama Canal and never a line nor a word of any kind to say why they have not. Oh, sir, can you put yourself for a moment in my poor parents' place . . . Perhaps you are a father yourself, if so think what it would mean to lose all trace of your loved one. My father and mother grieve sorely . . . Indeed this awful mystery is killing them slowly but surely.

It makes my heart bleed and cry out against the one who is causing them all this worry for they don't deserve it, for we have the best father and mother in the world and they were both to John Wilson, many a time I think too good and so prevented him from realizing his own responsibility. Only this morning I had a letter from my father and in it he says, "We have a very sad home now and one that used to be oh so happy. Surely God will cause someone to be able to give us news of my girl and I hope all will yet come right." Mr. Horrigan, *dare* I ask you to be the one to help them. God knows what I suffer in not knowing what has come over my sister for she and I were very dear to one another and for years were seldom separate.

Is my brother-in-law on your staff as Mr. Routledge said? Will you at least answer my letter. Oh, sir, I plead to you also for the sake of Mr. and Mrs. Wilson's two little ones who are always enquiring about their mammy to answer this letter and give us what information you may have. Indeed I plead with you for God's sake to do all in your power to help us to find them . . .

My husband bids me say he will more than gladly pay any expense you may be put to in acquiring news. Many a time poor father has said, "Oh, if I were able I would not sit here and wait for news, I would go to Canada and search it all over till I found Polly." Indeed my husband says if we don't get news soon he will try and get out himself before he will wait and see Father and Mother break their hearts. May God help you to bring at least peace if not joy to my folks.

> I remain, dear sir,
> Yours v. gratefully,
> E. Craig

At the same time she wrote to Assistant Commissioner Routledge, another long, impassioned letter, asking for his help: "Mr. Routledge, . . . did she and her husband go to Vancouver? Or has my brother-in-law gone and left my sister, breaking her heart for him in some corner, or, oh sir, is she dead? (My father maintains she is) . . . It is now fully 8 months since we received John Wilson's cable . . . Can you guess the preparations that were made and the children's daily anticipations of their arrival to be followed by this awful silence."

Elizabeth did not know that the two men she looked to for help were both seriously ill. Joseph Horrigan would soon take an extended leave and travel to Hawaii in an effort to get well; and Walton Routledge, whose health was failing even as he took on the added duties of assistant commissioner the previous January, would soon begin a six-month leave for the same purpose. From this point on, Commissioner Perry himself would reply to Elizabeth's ever more distraught letters.

A. Bowen Perry was a brilliant man with an illustrious career. Born in Ontario of United Empire Loyalist stock, he entered the Royal Military College at age sixteen where he won Governor General's gold and silver medals. Appointed inspector in the North West Mounted Police at age twenty-two, promoted to superintendent at twenty-five for services in the North West Rebellion, he was made commissioner of the force in 1900, at age forty. Perry was renowned for his prodigious memory for names and faces and for facts and figures, and also for his keen sense of justice and fairness.

Chapter xxx

⟶ AUTUMN ⟵

It is harvest time on the prairie. In all directions from the culvert, the land is brushed with gold, and the trees and bushes ablaze with colour. Cumbrous machinery lumbers between thick, glistening swaths, and field mice scurry for cover as sunburned threshers work late and long in the fragrant fields. Bushes either side of the culvert glow a deep red flecked with orange. The same wildflowers Polly Wilson admired on her last day on earth soak up the mellow autumn sun. And at night an immense red harvest moon hangs in the sky like a Chinese lantern.

Chapter xxxi

SOMETHING VERY FUNNY

At 138 Cordova Street in Vancouver's pawnshop/second-hand district, Mrs. Sissons sat behind the counter with her black-sweatered arms crossed over her ample bosom. There was hardly room there for so large a woman, hardly room anywhere in the store, cluttered to the ceiling with the detritus of people moving up or down in life. Business had been slow, and it was almost closing time. It was early October and the rain was falling for the fifth day in a row as if it never intended to stop. Outside, the dark was already closing in, a rising wind flinging the rain onto the windows in big wet gusts. Inside, half a wall of clocks ticked endlessly.

Mrs. Sissons was scanning the Classifieds in the newspaper on the counter when the bell tinkled. A man wearing a damp blue suit and grey hat threaded his way to the counter, knocking over a scrub board with his elbow, which in turn knocked over several other small items. Mrs. Sissons sighed.

"Would you be interested in buying a shotgun?" he asked, when he reached the counter.

"Sure. I just sold the last one yesterday. If it's in good condition, of course. You wouldn't believe the junk some people bring in here."

"It's in good condition, all cleaned and with a leather case."

"You have it here? I'm closing soon."

"No, I have to go home and get it. But it's not far. I'll be right back."

Mrs. Sissons glanced at the clocks on the wall, all more or less pointing to half past four.

"If you hurry, I'll wait."

At five o'clock he was back with a good-looking gun, made in Scotland, in a fine old country leather case, stamped with the initials JLW.

"How much do you want for it?" she asked, after giving it the once over. It was a double barrel, hammerless, in nice condition.

"Twenty-five dollars."

Not bad. Usually they made you work harder for it.

"Twenty-three," she said.

"I'll take it," he said.

She gave him the book to sign, the last entry on October 4, 1919. He wrote—"J. Williams, 1539 Robson Street"—and she gave him two limp tens and three ones.

She walked behind him to the door and locked it behind him. Ten days later she sold the gun to a Mr. Mutch, 2646 Yukon Street, for thirty-five dollars. Mutch. Strange name, that, Mrs. Sissons thought. If it *was* his name.

∽

The following letter is one of the last official letters written by Superintendent Fitzpatrick J. Horrigan. His health had deteriorated quickly, and in early November he obtained a six-month leave and travelled to Hawaii, where he hoped to recover his health. This letter would have been written before Elizabeth's letter, written in late September, arrived in Vancouver.

Vancouver, Oct. 10th, 1919

Confidential.

The Commissioner,

RNWM Police,

Regina, Sask.

Sir,

Re: #6020 Sergeant John L. Wilson

I have the honour to report that I am now through with the above named N.C.O. We have only three Russian cases remaining, and he has no evidence to tender in any of them. His work during the past month has not been very satisfactory to me, especially since I have been unwell and unable to follow up as closely as I should have liked.

I have no direct charge to place against Sergt. Wilson, but many of his actions did not appear good to me. As he is uncovered now, of course his further work here would be useless. I did think of sending him to the Prince Rupert district, but I rather lost confidence in him; hence I should be very pleased if you would wire me to transfer him to some other Division.

> I have the honour to be,
> Sir
> Your obedient servant,
> F. J. Horrigan, Supt.
> Commanding "E" Division

The commissioner's coded reply was succinct: "Your letter tenth. Send Sergeant Wilson to Regina for instructions."

In preparation, the Wilsons moved out of the Homer Street house and into the City Hotel. Jack knew he had real reason to worry now, but still he said nothing to Jessie.

On October 21, Inspector Henry Newson notified Commissioner Perry that Sergeant Wilson had been recalled by the Immigration Board to give evidence. They would advise the commissioner of Wilson's departure in a day or two.

These trials, often referred to as the "Russian trials," may have been Dukobor trials, but were more likely trials of radical extremists who were advocating the declaration of general strikes. The west was seething with labour troubles, with dissidents relying on a disaffected foreign element in the population for support. Waterfront hostilities were commonplace. Wilson gained the confidence of stevedores by drinking with them and kept his ears open for trouble that might be brewing.

His testimony given, Wilson was ordered to depart immediately for Regina, and he and Jessie left on a late train on October 23.

> REGINA, SASKATCHEWAN,
> OCTOBER 24, 1919

SUPERINTENDENT HORRIGAN,
RNWM POLICE,
VANCOUVER, B.C.
YOUR LETTER 21ST RE WILSON. HAVE YOU PHOTOGRAPH MRS

WILSON SENT BY CRAIG. IF SO FORWARD HERE. ADVISE BY
WIRE IF WOMAN LIVING WITH WILSON ACCOMPANIES HIM
WHEN HE LEAVES FOR REGINA.

A. B. PERRY, COMMISSIONER

The coded reply arrived on the commissioner's desk the same day,
signed by Inspector Newson, who, it appears, came from Victoria to
replace Superintendent Horrigan while he was on leave.

Inspector Newsom had joined the RNWMP in 1906. By 1910, at the
age of thirty, he had risen to the rank of inspector and was soon
responsible for visiting all divisional posts in Alberta and Saskatchewan and establishing a fingerprint system for RNWMP guard-
rooms. At six feet three inches tall, he had a commanding presence.

VANCOUVER, B.C.
OCTOBER 24, 1919

COMMISSIONER A. B. PERRY,
RNWM POLICE,
REGINA, SASK.

WILSON LEFT ON NUMBER EIGHT ON TWENTY THIRD STOP.
PARTY REFERRED TO YOUR CODE TELEGRAM OF TODAY LEFT
HOTEL WITH HIM STOP. PHOTOGRAPH IN HIS POSSESSION
STOP. REFER YOU TO LETTER OF THIRTY FIRST JULY.

H. M. NEWSON

Even as they travelled west, Jack still thought about running. At any
point along the route, they could get off the train. There was nothing
to stop them, but where would they go? He had no money to speak of;
the money from the old country had dried up long ago and there were
no MSA fines to turn to his advantage. They'd catch up with him
before long, and he hated to drag Jessie into it. At least in Saskatchewan she had her family to go to when it broke, and that was inevitable
now. And something in him had always known he would see the
whole thing through.

Jack and Jessie arrived in Regina and checked into the Grand
Hotel. Jack presented himself at headquarters and was told his

posting wasn't decided yet. They'd appreciate it if he would stay in Regina until they needed him, sometime in the next few days.

Shortly after his arrival, he was again recalled by the Immigration Board to give further evidence at one of the Russian trials. He left for Vancouver, leaving Jessie behind in the Grand Hotel.

Chapter XXXII

ᴄᴏ A SHADOWY PICTURE ᴄᴏ

On October 30, 1919, Staff Sergeant Herbert Darling from the Regina Depot Division, called at the Office of Vital Statistics, and in very short order held in his hand the marriage certificate of one John L. Wilson, Mounted Policeman, to Jessie Patterson of Blaine Lake on September 29, 1918.

He then drove to the Regina Burial Company, but found no record of the death of a Mrs. Wilson. Nor did Regina City Hospital have any record of her.

Then, through a connection of Mrs. Laing's whom he found in the phone book, Sergeant Darling contacted Thelma Wilson, Mrs. Laing's daughter and Polly's old school friend.

"I'm glad there's finally something being done about Polly," Thelma Wilson told him.

"Yes," her husband said. "We wrote to the police about it ourselves about three months ago but never heard anything."

"Do you know where Polly Wilson lived while she was in Regina?" Sergeant Darling asked.

"Yes, certainly," Thelma Wilson said eagerly. "It's a boarding house on Rose Street. I'll take you there if you like and introduce you to her landlady, Mrs. Wismer. She can tell you more than I can."

"Would you call and see if she can see us now?"

And soon they were seated in Eileen Wismer's dining room with the sliding oak doors closed for privacy. Eileen had set out tea and cookies. Sergeant Darling, a tall, dark, thirty-two-year-old Welshman, seemed an unlikely stenographer as he flipped open a notebook to record Eileen's observations. Eileen Wismer gratefully spilled out everything she could remember about Polly and Jack Wilson: how he treated her, never taking her anywhere public, and about Polly's discovery of Jessie Patterson's letter. She described the morning Polly left on the train at eight or nine o'clock, accompanied by Mrs. Hansen.

"She looked worried, as if she didn't want to go. She didn't know anybody in Saskatoon."

She talked about Polly's baby, due in January, and her promise to write, and she described Wilson's late night visit soon after she left.

"I thought it was strange, sending Polly off like that on her own when he planned to come down so soon himself. He took some mail for Polly."

"Did she receive a lot of mail?"

"Oh, yes. Every week she heard from the children in their own handwriting, and she was always writing to them and her family. Oh, she loved those children."

Sergeant Darling wrote energetically, funny little squiggles, slashes and dots all over the lined notebook. The late fall sun caught a bevelled mirror edge, reflecting a rainbow onto the white tablecloth.

"It's such a relief to be telling you this. I've been going over and over it in my head for a year now, I can't get those children out of my mind. Just last week I got a letter from Polly's sister, Nellie Hutchison. I haven't answered it yet. What could I say?"

"Do you have the letter?"

"Indeed, I do. It's right here." Eileen got up and retrieved a letter from a drawer in the sideboard. "Those poor people are nearly crazy with worry. Take it with you if you want to. I have the address."

"Thank you." Sergeant Darling pocketed the letter.

"Oh, and this pitiful one from Jack Wilson last winter, asking me to take Polly in. You can have that, too."

Sergeant Darling scanned the letter.

"I wrote him back and talked to him of religious matters, him being so near death and all. I should have known not to believe anything he said. I never trusted him, I'm sorry to say, even if he is a policeman."

Sergeant Darling smiled as he wrote that down.

"But I have every confidence in Mrs. Wilson. She is straightforward and honest as the day."

"Can you think of anything else, Mrs. Wismer?" Sergeant Darling asked.

"No, but I'm sure I will as soon as you're gone."

Darling closed the book and stood up. "Thank you, ma'am. You've been a great help."

They all stood chatting a moment in the sun-warmed veranda with its brown wicker chairs and wicker table piled with newspapers and magazines. Still-blooming geraniums lined the windowsills.

"Polly loved this room," Eileen Wismer said.

"We'd like you not to mention my being here to Sergeant Wilson, should you happen to receive a visit from him." Darling told her.

"Oh, don't worry," she replied. "I often had to play double with him so he wouldn't know I knew about their troubles. But I'd be hard put to be civil."

Eileen Wismer drew a huge breath of relief as she watched the sergeant walk down the sidewalk to his car, opening the door so courteously for Mrs. Wilson. At last something was being done—probably too late for Polly, she had a feeling—but at least they'd find out what happened.

༄

The day Sergeant Darling spoke to Mrs. Wismer, Superintendent C. H. West, Commanding Officer, "F" Division, Prince Albert, discovered Polly Wilson's trunks stored away at the Prince Albert express office. Commissioner Perry gave orders to have the trunks seized, and their contents listed.

One of the trunks contained bedding, a teapot, six silver spoons, cutlery, a small saucepan and jug, a pair of corsets, black woollen stockings, grey wool socks, a man's felt hat purchased in Regina and a few other sundries.

The other trunk revealed an RNWMP red serge tunic with corporal's chevrons, a field jacket and pea jacket, dress boots and spurs, felt hat, breeches and dress pants; a patchwork quilt, one flannelette and two cotton nightdresses; underskirt, and men's and women's shoes.

There were also two enlarged children's photos and a number of snapshots, which West judged to be taken in the Blaine Lake district, and the last letter Wilson wrote to Polly, instructing her to come to Saskatoon on September 27. West forwarded the letter and snapshots registered mail to Commissioner Perry.

∽

The night train from Regina arrived in Saskatoon at seven o'clock the next morning, and Sergeant Darling stepped off, eager to see what the day would produce. He wanted to talk to the occupants of 217 9th Street, Saskatoon, where Wilson's "next of kin Mary Wilson" had lived, according to Wilson's re-engagement papers. At the Saskatoon detachment, he found that a Mrs. Amelia Foster was the present resident at that address. Mrs. Foster confirmed by telephone that the Wilsons had lived with her the previous fall. Posing as an old friend of Jessie's, Sergeant Darling visited Mrs. Foster in the handsome three-storey house.

Whatever Mrs. Foster thought of another man's interest in Mrs. Wilson, and a tall, dark, handsome one at that, she didn't comment. She told him the Wilsons' arrival and departure dates, and the fact they were newly married when they came and were very happy.

"Do you have a photograph of Mrs. Wilson I could have?"

Mrs. Foster hesitated. "I'll see." And she produced one from an album in the sitting room.

Sergeant Darling studied the slim young woman in the photo. She was laughing, posed by a railing with her hair blowing. There were mountains in the background. He turned the photo over.

"Somewhere close to Banff, fondly, Jessie" was written on the back in a young woman's handwriting. Jackpot! he thought.

"That's a nice picture of her," he said. "I'll return it to you. Do you have an address for Jessie?"

"Yes. They left an oil stove and asked me to sell it. I did, for fifteen dollars, and sent the money to them in Vancouver." Another short search produced the address: 804 Homer Street.

Darling now had a photo of Wilson's new wife, a sample of her handwriting, and confirmation that she had lived with Jack Wilson at the Vancouver address.

Sergeant Darling next called at the Sutherland post office, where Eileen had written to Wilson care of Mrs. Clark. They had no box number for a Mrs. Clark. In fact, the only Mrs. Clark living in Sutherland had never heard of John or Polly Wilson. Sergeant Darling caught the 5:30 train back to Regina, arriving about 12:30 A.M.

Later that day, he typed the first "Confidential Crime Report, Enquiry re Mrs. M. Wilson"—the first of a great many.

Like a print in a developing tray, a shadowy picture was beginning to form.

Chapter XXXIII

∽ QUESTIONS, QUESTIONS, QUESTIONS ∾

People must have wondered what was going on. Suddenly there were policemen everywhere you looked. They fanned out from Regina, Saskatoon and Prince Albert detachments in every direction; it seemed on every train there were one or two Mounties, stepping off at various points to question hotel clerks, post office employees, men who had scattered around the province and into Alberta after the Military Police disbanded, doctors, automobile agents, express agents, landladies, boarders and many more. Letters, phone calls and telegrams flew back and forth between the Saskatchewan detachments, and crisscrossed the country between the prairies and the coast and to Polly's family in Scotland as the story unfolded.

At the New Windsor Hotel in Saskatoon, the desk clerk, who knew Wilson, pointed to a register entry for October 2, 1918: "J. Wilson and Wife."

"I know that woman well," the clerk said. "She is old man Patterson's daughter from Blaine Lake."

∾

"She bought a corsage in the train station the day she left for Saskatoon," Mrs. Hansen told Constable Chalk. "She was always careful with money, but I think she wanted to look nice for her husband. They had had some troubles and it was a new start for her."

"What sort of troubles did they have?"

"It was to do with another woman who lived at Blaine Lake. I never heard her last name, but her first name was Jessie."

On inquiry at the Sutherland post office, Sergeant C. J. Hildyard of the Saskatoon detachment learned that Wilson had rented Box 287 on October 19, 1918, paying a year's rent in advance. In the early part of 1919, the post master received a letter from Vancouver from Wilson, advising him to redirect all mail to General Delivery, Vancouver.

One of the Saskatoon "F" Division main investigators was Detective Sergeant Alexander Drysdale, a Scot, recently demobilized from the cavalry squadron. Sergeant Drysdale, a man of medium height with dark hair, grey-blue eyes and refined features, was described by Superintendent West, his commanding officer, as "an educated man and a gentleman in every sense of the word."

One of the people Sergeant Drysdale interviewed was Fred Burge. The two men sat on wooden crates drinking tea in the back of Burge's general store in Blaine Lake.

"Oh, yes, his first wife came over and caused a lot of trouble for him, or that's what his story was," Fred said.

"Oh? What kind of trouble?"

"She was as wild as a hare, I guess. You know, drinking, running around with men. He apparently couldn't do anything with her."

"What happened to her? Did she go back to Scotland?"

"No, she was killed in a car accident, and then he married a girl from here. John Patterson's daughter."

"How soon after the accident did he get married again?"

"Awful damned soon. It had people's tongues wagging, I can tell you."

Interesting, thought Drysdale.

Back in Saskatoon that afternoon, Sergeant Drysdale bumped into W. C. Craig, an ex-stoker at the Battleford RNWMP who had served in the Military Police under Wilson at Saskatoon.

"I wish I had time to talk over old times, but I'm on the next train to North Battleford," Craig told him.

"I'll go with you," Drysdale said.

On the train ride, Craig confirmed Wilson's marriage to Jessie. "We were all glad, since he spent all his time at Blaine Lake. And we figured it'd cut down on his boozing."

"Did it?"

"Not much. But at least he was around. And then he was AWOL for quite awhile, or we thought he was, but it turned out he had a bad case of flu out in the country somewhere. Say, did you know Gillis, who went overseas with the cavalry unit?"

Drysdale was looking at the dry snowflakes drifting past the train windows and onto the fields and bluffs. Snow made finding a grave a whole lot harder. It made everything harder.

He shook his head. "No, I didn't. Why?"

"He lives at Blaine Lake and could probably tell you more about what went on out there."

Sergeant Drysdale caught the next train from North Battleford to Blaine Lake.

Back in Blaine Lake, Sergeant Drysdale talked to Mr. Gillis over a cup of coffee in the local Chinese café. Aware of the other patrons' interest in their conversation, they kept their voices low.

"Yes, his first wife was supposed to have come to Regina before he married the Patterson girl."

"What happened to her? The first wife?"

"Well, he put out the story that she died in a car accident. But when he married Jessie right away, people said that his wife died very conveniently for him."

"Was she ever in Blaine Lake?"

"You mean the first Mrs. Wilson? No, no one around here ever saw her. I guess he kept her away from here."

"Can you tell me anything else about it?"

"Not really. Jessie Patterson was a lot younger than Wilson and some said she did most of the courting."

"Did the second Mrs. Wilson know about the first one?"

Gillis shrugged. "I don't know that she knew. People said she believed he was divorced. Maybe she thought his divorced wife came chasing after him. Who knows what he told her."

Indeed, thought Sergeant Drysdale.

"Anyway, most of that talk went on after they were married and away from here. I don't suppose her folks would tell her."

"Perhaps not. Where can I find Mr. Patterson?"

"Right across the street in the livery stable. He's usually there."

Drysdale met Jessie's father, but just chatted about things in general, before catching a train to Saskatoon. His orders were to catch the morning train to Regina.

∾

Telegraph keys were clacking, typewriters clattering, phone lines buzzing. Number 6020, Sergeant John Wilson, the cause of all this commotion, was on a train back to Vancouver to give more evidence at "one of the Russian trials." Jessie stayed behind at the Grand Hotel in Regina.

REGINA, SASK.,
NOV. 2, 1919

SIXTY TWENTY LEFT HERE FOR VANCOUVER SATURDAY NIGHT. STOP. MATTER REFERRED TO HORRIGAN'S LETTER JULY THIRTY FIRST VERY SUSPICIOUS. HE IS NOT AWARE INVESTIGATION BEING MADE.

A. B. PERRY

The day Jack left, Jessie wired her mother to come to Regina. Mrs. Patterson wired back that she couldn't come, and suggested Jessie come home to Blaine Lake. But Jessie stayed in Regina, anxiously waiting for Jack's return.

∾

Sergeant Hildyard paid a visit to Mr. Riddell, the Grey Dort dealer. Riddell described the accident that happened, he thought, on September 27, a couple of days before Wilson came in with his new wife.

"He told me the government was going to pay for the new car. He only had to go to Regina and sign a requisition. So he asked for fifteen days to pay. I went to the bank with him and that's what he told the banker, too."

"Where did the accident happen?"

"Out near the Borden Ferry somewhere. The two men who went out there to haul in the burned car don't work here any more. That was Southey and Walt Kelland, but I can tell you where they are now."

Hildyard also spoke to Riddell's secretary, Jean Brown, who said that Wilson had introduced Jessie and said they were married the day before.

"He looked ready to jump out of his skin the whole time they were here. In fact, I thought he might be sick," she said.

ᨆ

On another visit to Rose Street, Sergeant Darling heard from Eileen Wismer that after finding Jessie's letter, Polly felt "very bad." She spent most of her time in her room, preparing light meals on an oil stove there. She blamed herself for her troubles, for not coming to Canada sooner. When Eileen had asked if her family knew of her troubles, she said they did not, and that she'd rather do anything than bring disgrace on her family.

ᨆ

In Vancouver, Jack Wilson wasn't sleeping well. He sent the following message at 2:34 A.M. on November 4:

VANCOUVER, B.C.
NOV. 4, 1919

MRS. JOHN WILSON
HOTEL GRAND
REGINA SASK
LEAVING HERE TOMORROW NIGHT FOR REGINA DID NOT KNOW SOONER WIRE ME IF MOTHER HAS ARRIVED I WILL

TELEGRAPH AGAIN IN THE MORNING
JACK
Copy made for RNWMP

Wilson's telegram to ask if her mother had arrived seems to indicate that Mrs. Patterson was needed for something more important than a pleasant family visit.

～

REGINA, SASK.
4TH NOV. 1919

ELIZABETH CRAIG
TINTO VIEW
KILNCADZOW
CARLUKE (SCOTLAND)
JUST DISCOVERED WILSON RE-MARRIED SEPTEMBER 29, 1918. SECOND WIFE MISTAKEN FOR YOUR SISTER. NO TRACE MARY WILSON SINCE SEPTEMBER NINETEEN EIGHTEEN. GRAVE SUSPICIONS. SEARCH ENERGETICALLY CONTINUED. SEND CERTIFICATE MARRIAGE.

A. B. PERRY
COMMISSIONER
MOUNTED POLICE

REGINA, SASK.
NOVEMBER 4, 1919

INSPECTOR H. M. NEWSON
RNWM POLICE
CREDIT FONCIER BUILDING
VANCOUVER, B.C.
CODED MESSAGE.
SIXTY TWENTY MUST BE CLOSELY WATCHED. MATTER NOW LOOKS VERY SERIOUS. ADVISE HOW LONG HE WILL BE REQUIRED VANCOUVER.

A. B. PERRY

REGINA, SASK.
NOV. 5, 1919
CODED MESSAGE.
HAVE YOU 6020 COVERED. IMMEDIATE REPLY REQUIRED
EXPLAIN DELAY ANSWERING MY WIRE NOV. 4TH.
A. B. PERRY

VANCOUVER B.C.
5TH NOV. 1919
THE COMMISSIONER,
RNWM POLICE,
REGINA, SASK.
OUR CIPHER FIFTH STOP SIXTY TWENTY COVERED STOP
UNABLE STATE YET WHEN HE CAN RETURN. WILL NOTIFY
YOU BY WIRE STOP FORWARDING EXPLANATION.
H. M. NEWSON

Inspector Newson's "personal and confidential" explanation, written the same day, informed the commissioner that Sergeant J. Fripps had been detailed to keep Sergeant Wilson under observation. He apologized for not answering Perry's wire of November 4, but had been waiting for something definite to report.

ᴖ

In the little town of Ardath, south of Saskatoon, Walt Kelland talked to Constable Chalk about the burned car he had hauled into Saskatoon a little over a year ago. He recounted the trip to the culvert with Jack Wilson and his new wife, and the dinner Wilson bought as a little wedding celebration. He supplied exact directions and drew a map to the culvert.

ᴖ

In Vancouver, Sergeant Cather received a telegram on November 5:

REGINA, SASK.

NOVEMBER 5, 1919

LET ME KNOW AT ONCE IF SGT. WILSON LEFT WEDNESDAY FOR REGINA.

MRS. J. WILSON

HOTEL GRAND

Sergeant Cather handed Jessie's wire to Inspector Newson. Newson looked at it and gazed out the window for a few moments. It was a still, dark day, the sky low and leaden.

"Wire her back and tell her he didn't leave Wednesday, but that he's leaving tomorrow."

"Yes, sir."

"He isn't leaving tomorrow, but if she's suspicious an investigation is being made, she may try to warn him."

"When do you think he will leave, sir?"

"Day after tomorrow, I hope, on the night train. He's in bed today with a severe case of hemorrhoids." Inspector Newsom raised his eyebrows and Sergeant Cather smiled.

"Will the trial be over then?"

"No, but the commissioner asked that Wilson not testify at the perjury trial, for obvious reasons, so our lawyer had his evidence placed in open court. Sergeant Fripps will accompany him to Regina."

"It will be interesting to follow this one, sir."

"It will indeed, Sergeant. It will indeed."

Chapter xxxiv

⟿ SOMEONE OTHER THAN MRS. WILSON ⟿

On November 6, 1919, Sergeant Drysdale asked the new express agent in Prince Albert for information regarding Polly Wilson's trunks. The agent wired Ned Storie at the Great Northern Express in

Edmonton. Storie replied that Mrs. Wilson had advised them around the end of November 1918 that she was in Sutherland Hospital with the flu, and asked them to hold the trunks till she was able to call or send for them. She also asked what charges were against them. Storie had promptly sent an invoice but heard nothing further from Mrs. Wilson. Storie concluded by saying that if no hospital record could be found for her, he presumed that someone other than Mrs. Wilson wrote to the express office regarding the trunks.

_∾_

Commissioner Perry knew he wouldn't rest easy until Number 6020 was safely back in Regina. The possibility of Wilson bolting was very much on his mind, and he worried there might be a slip-up in Vancouver. He also wanted an officer he knew personally to accompany Wilson back to Saskatchewan.

REGINA, SASK.,
NOVEMBER 7, 1919

INSPECTOR H. M. NEWSON,
RNWM POLICE,
VANCOUVER, B.C.
WHEN IS SIXTY TWENTY LEAVING. WROTE YOU YESTERDAY REGARDING ADVISABILITY NOT USING HIM AS WITNESS PERJURY CASES. SERGT. THOMAS TRANSFERRED DEPOT AND IS TO TRAVEL WITH SIXTY TWENTY AND TAKE EVERY PRECAUTION AGAINST HIS DISAPPEARANCE.
A. B. PERRY

Sergeant Wilson and Sergeant Thomas boarded the eastbound night train on November 7. Like Wilson, Sergeant Thomas was a Scot in his thirties. He'd emigrated to Canada in 1908 after eight years in the British Army, and like so many others involved in the Wilson investigation, he had served with the RNWMP's cavalry overseas. The two men wore identical uniforms, but the six-foot-tall, fair-haired Thomas looked fit and at ease, while Wilson looked pale and strained, his uniform too large for him now. His posture was still straight, but he walked carefully, like a man in pain. (Something else Wilson and Thomas shared was a fondness for the bottle. Thomas's energy and hard work would be rewarded with a promotion to inspector early in 1920. Then, guilty of intoxication, he would be transferred to Ottawa the following June and, convicted on the same charge soon after, dismissed from the force.)

As the train steamed west, Jack had a lot of time to think. He knew that when he got to Regina he'd be interrogated about Polly's disappearance and his marriage to Jessie. It was strange: he could have written Polly's family that she had died of the flu. They'd have believed that, and possibly no one would have demanded a death certificate with so many deaths at the time. Why hadn't he? He didn't know himself. Nor had he got rid of the dispatch bag and his incriminating letters to Jessie. His behaviour seemed foolhardy, even to himself. Still, unless he confessed or they found Polly's body, they couldn't charge him with murder.

He played cards with Sergeant Thomas and they talked about the old country and compared experiences, but as they drew nearer Saskatchewan, Wilson grew silent, and his glances strayed often to the passing landscape. Jessie had been so excited by her first sight of the mountains.

Green grass and mountains gave way to bare foothills, and finally the grey, dun and faded blue of the prairies. In Saskatchewan, ground-drifting snow obliterated the roads in places, swirled over the frozen ponds and striped black summer-fallow fields with waving white lines, like a carelessly drawn music staff on a blackboard.

Sergeant Thomas lounged against the wall nearby when Wilson went to the washroom, and Wilson felt his alertness as he paced the aisle to give some relief to his inflamed hemorrhoids. He also understood the sergeant's glance in his direction when he himself came out of the washroom. And when Jack awoke from sleeping so soundly he might have been dead, Thomas was sitting across from him, wide awake.

They didn't need to worry. He wasn't going anywhere. On the long journey, the mournful cry of the train whistle echoed his empty feeling over and over.

Polly's family was now even more distraught. They had been told about Wilson's marriage, but no news of Polly, except that no one had seen or heard from her since she left for Saskatoon.

> Tinto View
> Kilncadzow, Carluke
> Lanarkshire, Scotland
> 7th November 1919

Mr. A. B. Perry

Dear Sir:

We received your cable yesterday and I think, Sir, the news it contains has nearly given me my death blow and what it means to my Dear Father and Mother is more than I dare think. Both my husband and I were too upset to write yesterday.

Let me thank you for your great kindness in cabling the news as soon as you found how matters stood. We have known since March that there was something far wrong but never thought for a moment that Wilson was so bad at heart as to abandon my sister in a strange land. Has he committed bigamy? For surely he would not be guilty of foul play to his wife—the mother of his two children. I will enclose her marriage licence and will give you all other information that I can. [The letter goes on for pages, giving every detail of their efforts to contact Polly, and enclosing the cables and the letter from Wilson to her husband Archie.] . . .

I will know that if Wilson deserted her she would think shame and hide in her grief. She would not want to bring sorrow to Father and Mother, but, oh, not knowing where she is is a much greater sorrow to them . . .

God help this poor woman if he married her and she does not know him. She can't be happy with such a scoundrel for God will surely punish him and yet he is the father of two of the nicest wee children that ever lived.

Mr. Perry, will you please cable when you find her for it takes a letter so long to come. We will be only too pleased to pay all expenses if only we could bring back to happiness and joy my father and mother's lives.

Again thanking you for your kindness and thoughtfulness to us and also convey our thanks to Mr. Routledge for his kindness.

I remain, Dear Sir,
Yours v. gratefully
Elizabeth P. Craig

The day before Elizabeth wrote to Perry, Walton Routledge died on a train near Portland, Oregon. He was en route to California for his health, and he left a wife and three young children.

∽

G. S. Jobin, ex-accountant for the Military Police in Saskatoon, was happy to tell Sergeant Drysdale all about his service under Sub-Inspector Jack Wilson. Jobin worked in the money order office at the post office, where they sat down to talk.

"Wilson wasn't well known here, you know. He was out of town most of the time, but I had my private opinion of him," Jobin said.

"And what was that?"

"I thought he was a rum customer. You know, always up to something. I kept the books about the MSA fines collected, and his seemed to be off more often than not."

"Did you ever report it?"

"No. I didn't have any proof, and he was the boss, you know. Conrad Read was hand in glove with Wilson—they were great boozing partners. I think he could throw some light on the matter for you—if he will."

"Do you know where Read is now?"

"I think he's with your outfit out in Vancouver. He thought Wilson was 'just it,' but I thought he was a rum customer, and nothing he did ever changed my mind."

That night, in a handwritten note to Commissioner Perry, Sergeant Drysdale wrote: "The term 'hand in glove' is usually used in one way only, and I am mentioning it, so that if it is decided to interview Read (and it seems essential) the knowledge of intimacy between the two could be borne in mind."

In the back of Albert's Café, a favourite meeting place in Saskatoon,

Sergeant Drysdale took time for lunch as he talked to James Martin, who had also worked under Wilson in the Military Police.

"I was transferred from Regina and was senior man around the place," Martin said. "Inspector Wilson was drinking heavily all this time. He was going to Blaine Lake right along to see his sweetheart and the work was going to the devil."

The waitress refilled their cups with strong coffee and set apple pie, the day's dessert, in front of them.

"Was he drinking on the job, do you think?"

"I don't think, I know. Once he called Matthews and me into the washroom at the Armoury and asked us to drink to his upcoming marriage. I remember it well. He had a flask inside his tunic."

Martin also recounted in detail the trip out to the burned car. "I walked through the culvert that day, walking almost upright," he said. "The grass was about a foot and a half long in there, and I remember the slough was almost dry but muddy."

"Is there anything else you remember around the time of the accident?"

"Nothing important. But Sergeant Read was an intimate of Inspector Wilson's and would know all about his movements at the time."

∾

As Constable Chalk of the Saskatoon detachment gassed up his car at the gas station used by the Military Police, he asked the proprieter if he remembered Wilson. William Batchelor did, and furthermore, he remembered Wilson buying gas on the last Friday in September last year, and said he was on his way to his wedding.

"On Saturday or Sunday he came in again, and said he had not been able to get a parson. I can't recall if he told me this or if I heard him say it on the phone."

The picture in the developing tray was subtly changing: a shadowy image emerging here, another taking shape over there.

The Mounties were now convinced that Jack Wilson had committed murder, and they suspected Polly Wilson's body was buried somewhere in the vicinity of the burned car. They investigated a well near the culvert, and Constable Chalk reported that it was "merely a sunk hole in the slough, with some cribbing around it, which had not been tampered with." They did not dig under the culvert. Long grass and weeds grew there, and James Martin had stated this was also the case at the time of Wilson's accident.

Drysdale also talked to Charles McLean, who had visited Blaine Lake with Wilson and their wives shortly after Wilson's wedding. He recalled that when they passed by the burned car on the way, Wilson had told him that he tried to fight the fire with his overcoat, burning the coat but not putting out the fire. McLean said that Wilson took the burning of the car pretty easily. "He showed no worry or nervousness," McLean said.

If the police subscribed to the theory that the perpetrator revisits the scene of the crime, then this would seem to be it. Wilson couldn't stay away from the place. He had visited the culvert the week after the accident at least twice with his new wife, and could have done so alone any number of times.

He showed no worry or nervousness, McLean said. Nor, judging by his actions then and later, did he feel any remorse.

∿

Finally, on Sunday, November 10, the conductor called out, "Regina. Next stop Regina," and the train squealed and huffed and finally jarred to a stop.

As a pale Jack Wilson stepped off the train into a chill wind, he saw the car with two men from the barracks waiting. If they were concerned he might make a break for it, he would set their minds at ease. He walked briskly to the car, his back very straight, climbed in the back seat and smartly shut the door. Sergeant Thomas got in the other side.

At headquarters he was read a discipline charge involving complaints about the way he had handled witnesses in one of his undercover Vancouver investigations. And then this pronouncement: "John Lindsay Wilson, you are dismissed from the service of the Royal North West Mounted Police as of November 7, 1919."

He was led away to the guardroom.

Assistant Commissioner Walton Routledge is seated at left in white pants and straw hat.
PHOTO: RCMP #4171

Superintendent Fitzpatrick J. Horrigan, RNWMP commanding officer in Vancouver.
PHOTO: RCMP #3866

Commissioner A. Bowen Perry (second from right, front row), with the Prince of Wales (centre) in 1919. In his long career, Perry served in the North West Mounted Police, the Royal North West Mounted Police and the Royal Canadian Mounted Police. He ushered in the modern era of the force. PHOTO: SASKATCHEWAN ARCHIVES BOARD

RNWMP guardroom, Regina, the scene of a macabre suicide attempt.
PHOTO: NATIONAL
ARCHIVES OF CANADA

Superintendent Charles Augustus Mahony, the man who raided police forces across the country to form the new Saskatchewan Provincial Police in just twenty-one days. PHOTO: SASKATCHEWAN ARCHIVES

Assistant Superintendent William Tracey (fourth from left with cane). Nothing much got past this laconic Scot. PHOTO: COURTESY OF LYNN HUDSON

Road from Saskatoon to Blaine Lake, with two figures standing at the left by the culvert. PHOTO: COURTESY OF LYNN HUDSON

Police officer and two local men digging for the body. PHOTO: COURTESY OF LYNN HUDSON

The body encased in frozen earth after removal from its shallow grave. PHOTO: COURTESY OF LYNN HUDSON

The body being removed from the site for shipment to Saskatoon. PHOTO: COURTESY OF LYNN HUDSON

Chief Justice Sir Frederick Haultain, who presided at the sensational murder trial.
PHOTO: SASKATCHEWAN ARCHIVES BOARD

The Prince Albert jail in 1920. A new jail was built in 1923. PHOTO: FRANK ANDERSON

Chapter xxxv

∽ A HIGHLY NERVOUS CONDITION ∾

A few hours later, as he suspected, the real purpose of the trip became clear. He stood shivering across the desk from Inspector Prime, with Sergeant Darling seated to his right, a shorthand pad open. The window behind the inspector's desk framed a stiff, leaden November day. Wilson's legs trembled.

Inspector Prime, a tall, thin man with strong features, looked at him in silence for what seemed like an eternity. Then it began.

"What has happened to your wife, Mrs. Mary Wilson? Her relatives in Scotland have been extremely worried about her."

"I don't know where she is."

"Why don't you know?"

"We quarrelled the day she arrived from the old country and I haven't seen her since."

"Oh? When was that?"

"Almost the end of September last year. The twenty-seventh of September, I think."

"And where did this . . . quarrel take place?" Inspector Prime asked drily.

"Right there on the station platform in Saskatoon."

Sergeant Darling wrote industriously.

"What happened then?"

"She just walked away. I don't know where she went."

Inspector Prime leaned back in his chair, crossing his long arms over his chest.

"And so September 27, 1918, was the last time you saw your wife, Mary Wilson, is that correct?"

"Yes."

"And you married Jessie Patterson of Blaine Lake on"—he brought his chair forward to consult some notes on his desk—"September 29, 1918?"

They both looked at Wilson. He suddenly felt extremely agitated.

"I did. And it was legal. I started the divorce proceedings before I left the old country, and they sent the papers here."

"Oh? Can you produce those papers?"

Sergeant Darling's pencil was loud in the silence. Then it stopped.

"Wilson, answer the question. Can you produce the divorce decree?"

"It's a long story." His lips trembled, his hands opened and shut. "Lots of family troubles enter in it. I want to make a written statement."

"Certainly. Sergeant Darling, please escort the prisoner back to the guardroom and provide him with what he needs."

And so he was taken back to the guardroom, a writing pad and pencil were placed on the table, and the door locked. Jack Wilson sat down to write.

It was terribly cold. There was no heat in the guardroom. He could not stop coughing, a deep, rattling cough, and his hemorrhoids were deeply painful. He pushed his hands into his jacket pockets to warm them before he started to write. There was a hole in the right-hand pocket, and pushing through it, his hand closed on something hard that had fallen into the jacket lining. He pulled it up into the pocket and felt the smooth surface of a penknife he'd lost some time back. He held it in his hand until it warmed. Shivering, he dropped the knife back into the bottom of his jacket and picked up the pencil.

Statement of Reg. No. 6020 Sergeant Wilson, J.

On New Years' day, 1908, I married Mary (Polly) Hutchison of Slamannan, Stirlingshire. My parents were both dead and had left me considerable money. I invested all this money then, in a field of glasshouses and went into the tomato raising business, and she lived with me in one of my late Father's houses. Her brother then came into the business which was extended considerably and as he had only a little money to invest then trouble commenced between he and I and many times between her and I. I worked night and day until June 1912. I booked a passage to Saskatoon on a Monday and sailed the next Saturday.

Arriving in Saskatoon I worked on a Bridge and Building gang until the next Spring when I quit and was employed as a gardener by the city until late fall, then I went on a piece of land near Prince Albert and started a small garden and got hailed out the first summer just a few weeks before the war started so I had to give it up. Then I went on a farm when the war started and immediately went to Prince Albert to enlist, but was rejected by the Doctor. About two weeks later I saw the RNWM Police advertise for men, and thinking they would go overseas, I went before the Doctor at Prince Albert and was accepted.

I worked very hard on the force and was sent to Blaine Lake Detachment in July 1915 and did duty there trying always to do my best. During all this time I had nothing to do with girls until the fall of 1916 when I became acquainted with Jessie Patterson. She was always so good to me above everybody else. The friendship continued during 1917 and I tried again to get overseas, as I realized it was becoming quite serious, then I took sick with tuberculosis and took my discharge from the Force on 31st August of that year. I was very sick all that winter and Jessie Patterson looked after me and was very kind to me even when stories were going around that I was a married man and then was a better friend than ever. She was absolutely pure and innocent in all this, and many many nights I lay awake in bed trying to make up my mind to leave her for her sake but I think I was not right in my mind by this time and remained in Blaine Lake until April 1918.

I then went to Prince Albert to enlist in the RNWMP Cavalry draft and was rejected by the doctors at Prince Albert. There I learned that my first wife was in Regina. I met her at Saskatoon and here I behaved the worst, but my mind could not have been right because we stayed in a room at Regina but did not get along together and I was very little there and could not keep away from Jessie Patterson. I was working for the Dominion [Military] Police at this time, having started at the beginning of May 1919 and was very soon made Sub-Inspector as I worked in the office early and late to be away from the other woman. She knew all about Jessie Patterson as I told her all about her and how good she had been to me when I was alone and sick.

Although I believe I was out of my mind then I was clever and cunning and God alone knows how I told lies to Jessie and she was so confident that she believed everything. I could not stay away from her and when she moved to Prince Albert I could not stay away from there, doing everything I could for her to make her happy but doing wrong in not staying away from her.

About the beginning of September I was made the offer of chief inspector, but knowing that I was not fit for it, I rejected the offer and was sent to Saskatoon early in September to take charge of that sub-district.

I wrote from Saskatoon when I arrived there, telling my first wife to come and I would meet her at Colonsay, then the morning she left, I phoned her to come to Saskatoon instead, that was on the last Friday in September 1918.

I worked that forenoon at the office then in the afternoon I met the train with the car I had purchased from Erskine in Regina, and we went out in the country. I was dazed and I have only a faint recollection of what happened but she died on the way. [Here Wilson wrote a line and then painstakingly crossed it out.] Then I went around to Blaine Lake and stayed there until Sunday. Jessie and I were married Sunday night in Saskatoon and from that day I did everything a man could to make her happy. I was afraid every hour that I would be arrested and wired Mrs. Wismer from Saskatoon that everything was all right and wired from Prince Albert when I was sick to send the trunks there.

There I was very ill with influenza and on getting better I came to Regina and re-engaged with the RNWMP. From that day Jessie was made as happy as she could possibly be. I got her everything she had a liking for and spent an awful lot of money taking her with me out west, dreading every day I would be in trouble. I seemed to get more cunning every day and, although dazed and weary, kept Jessie happy.

God knows I did this lassie wrong but every minute of the fourteen months I was with her were happiness to me in spite of my worry. I had to see her today and say good-bye and almost the last words she said were "I trust you, husband." She is far above any girl I ever met, honest, true and kind and she never knew what I had to do to gain her. I had it in my mind that I must marry her legally and I did it.

Jessie, this is near the end and when you read this it was my love for you all this, and Dearest Wee Wifie, although I have ruined your life it was done for love of you, now you know what I was worrying about many times when you asked me, better for you had I never met you and you may have got the life's happiness you deserved for your kindness.

This further certifies that my wee girlie never dreamt but what I had got a proper divorce. She many, many a time asked me for her papers, meaning the divorce papers.

Sgd. John Wilson

Trembling with exhaustion, he lay down on the cot and stared at the ceiling.

After a while, Jack got up and went back to the table, walking bent and stiff, like an old man, and picked up the pencil:

P.S. Father and Mother, be merciful to Jessie. She is not to blame for the terrible shock this will give you when you hear that I have brought shame on your girlie Jessie.

Sgd. John Wilson

◌

In the small hours of the morning the prisoner still hadn't slept. He began to cough and couldn't stop, sitting up on the edge of the cot, coughing and coughing till he spat up blood. He got up and looked at the statement, then took the knife from his pocket and lay down again.

Around 4:00 A.M. he pushed the point of the blade into his throat on the left side, and made a little cut. Oddly, he felt no pain. He was very shaky, and he steadied his right hand with his left as he cut the gash wider. Blood poured down and around his neck. He stopped and lay still for awhile. Then he raised the knife again, steadied his hand once more, and opened the wound several more inches. His arm fell limp, still holding the knife.

Suddenly his head cleared. What had he done? He didn't want to die. Blood kept coming into his throat, making it hard to swallow. He put his hand up inside the wound and felt what he had done, felt his pulse beating wetly in his hand. He should tell the guard but he didn't want to because they would have to get the doctor out of bed. He would wait till morning. The corporal would be in at seven o'clock.

◌

Corporal Hutchinson thought Wilson was dead, lying there with his eyes closed, white as the driven snow except for the blood, the ghastly jagged gash from ear to ear, oozing bright fresh blood on top of darker dried blood, his shirt collar and the top of the blanket soaked with it.

"Here," said Wilson, scaring Corporal Hutchinson half out of his wits. "Here." Holding out the bloody penknife with a pale blood-stained hand. Then Wilson smiled at him.

Corporal Hutchinson never forgot it.

Nov. 11th/19

To the Commissioner,
RNWMP
Sir:

Re Prisoner Wilson

I have the honour to report that I was called early this morning to see the above named prisoner who had cut his throat very severely. Fortunately no large vessels were cut. I dressed the wound and sent him by ambulance to General Hospital. As a number of muscles in neck are cut an operation will be performed this morning. The wound is about seven inches long. I will therefore be unable to be at orderly-room.

> I have the honour to be
> Sir
> Your obedient servant
> T. A. Morrison
> Surgeon

On November 12, Commissioner Perry wrote to the RNWMP comptroller in Ottawa, giving a complete report of the Wilson case. As this was now a matter for which a criminal charge would be laid, he notified the comptroller that the investigation would be handed over to Superintendent Charles Mahony, head of the Saskatchewan Provincial Police, together with an offer of cooperation on the part of the RNWMP. He pointed out to the comptroller that Wilson did not re-engage with the force until January 6, 1919—three months after the suspected crime was committed. As soon as Wilson could be moved, he would be transferred to the provincial jail, with criminal charges preferred against him by the provincial authorities.

On November 11, Inspector Prime, following Commissioner Perry's instructions, turned over a copy of the complete file—"Mary Wilson, Missing"—to Superintendent Mahony. He also forwarded a cardboard box containing letters, papers and photographs found in Polly Wilson's trunks. A new cast of players was about to step on stage.

But the old ones were not rushing for the wings. On November 13, Commissioner Perry wrote to Superintendent Horrigan, requesting that "Agent #35," Conrad Read, be interviewed regarding Wilson's personal family affairs and any light he could throw on the car accident: "Secure this information with the least possible delay."

Then, on November 13, the newspapers broke the story.

Chapter xxxvi

_↷_ READ ALL ABOUT IT! _↶_

On November 13, 1919, the Saskatoon *Daily Star* reported:

SENSATIONAL MURDER CASE IS SUSPECTED
Police Closely Searching Country Near Borden Ferry For Woman's Body
JOHN WILSON TRIES SUICIDE
Believed That He Killed His Wife And Married Another Two Days Later

John Wilson is lying at death's door in Regina General Hospital, having slashed his own throat, and police are making a close search for the body of Mary Wilson, who died in an automobile Sept. 27, 1918, according to her husband's statement.

Wilson is charged with attempted suicide. Police believe the body of his dead wife must be somewhere in the vicinity of the Borden Ferry. Mary out of the way, John Wilson married Jessie Patterson of Blaine Lake, two days later.

Thus began the public love affair with the John Wilson murder case.

It was a sensation, no other word for it. Newspapers flew off the stands and out of the hands of paper boys. In every café, street corner, and around every supper table the talk was of Sergeant John

Wilson and the poor woman who came all the way from Scotland only to end up in an unmarked grave somewhere out there. It was the love triangle—and the fact that John Wilson was a policeman—that made it so irresistible. And *two days* later, he married the other woman!

∾

On the day the story broke, Commissioner Perry wrote to Elizabeth Craig. He described in detail the events that eventually led up to Wilson's arrest and attempted suicide. Then he went on:

> I regret to have to inform you that the suspicions against John Wilson in connection with the disappearance of his wife, Mary Wilson, are now very grave indeed. In his written statement, John Wilson states that his wife, Mary Wilson, died in his car, in which he took her out in the country after her arrival at Saskatoon.
>
> It is with the deepest regret that I have to advise you that from the facts as disclosed by our exhaustive investigations and the statement of Wilson, that your sister, Mary Wilson, apparently met her death at his hands on September 27, 1918. I might state that so far Wilson has not given any details regarding the crime, neither has he yet disclosed what disposition was made of the body.
>
> Please accept my deepest sympathy for yourself and Mrs. Wilson's family in this sad affair; and I should like to assure you that every possible effort is being made to ascertain the exact details and place the guilt for this crime upon the party responsible, after which, no effort will be spared to bring him to justice.

To get the news to the family sooner, the next day Commissioner Perry sent the following cable.

REGINA, SASK.
NOV. 14TH, 1919.

ELIZABETH CRAIG,
KILNCADZOW,
CARLUKE, SCOTLAND.

WILSON STATES WIFE DIED NOVEMBER NINETEEN EIGHTEEN.
HELD ON CHARGE MURDER. ATTEMPTED SUICIDE.

A. B. PERRY

MOUNTED POLICE

The date of death given as November was an error on someone's part and would cause even more confusion and grief in Polly's family.

∽

Now there were not only RNWMP officers everywhere, there were also SPP officers investigating the disappearance of Mary Wilson. The Saskatchewan Provincial Police, under the astute guidance of Charles Augustus Mahony, had in just two years become a highly respected police force.

Charles Mahony was very much his own man. As inspector of criminal investigation for the Ontario Provincial Police, he preferred to work in plainclothes and resigned when uniforms became mandatory. A strong Liberal and Roman Catholic, he could not be swayed by influential politicians, was fair in his dealings and was able to enforce discipline without using an iron hand. Many ex-Mounties, on returning from the war, chose to join its ranks rather than return to the RNWMP.

The SPP uniform was a long khaki tunic (better than the Mounties' "bum freezer," they said), with high, military collar, khaki breeches with a red stripe down the side, brown boots and leggings, and a brown Stetson hat with the brim turned up on the left side similar to the South African bushman's hat. Officers wore peaked caps and lapel-collared tunics.

Mahony knew his hastily organized force lacked the flair of its counterparts, with no spirited bands, musical ride, public relations men, famous red-coated uniforms and no glowing reports in the press. Without any of these trappings, their reputation for quiet efficiency steadily grew.

Compared to the Mounties, life in the SPP was informal. Members saluted their officers and members of the legislature but, as one SPP veteran put it, "one salute would do." Officers were easily available to the men. That same veteran said, "You could talk to your officers in the Provincial Police, discuss things with them."

But Charles Mahony insisted on one thing. As soon as they received word of a crime, they were to investigate while the clues were hot. In the case of "Mary Wilson, Missing," the clues were almost fourteen months old.

The first joint investigation took place on November 14. Detective Sergeant Drysdale teamed up with Sergeant Sparkman, SPP, and James Martin, civilian, and drove to the culvert. (Martin had worked under Wilson in the Military Police and accompanied him to the burned car after his wedding.)

At Rosthern, the two policemen interviewed Isaac Neufeldt, the farmer who first saw Wilson the morning of September 28, 1918. Neufeldt told them in detail everything that happened from the time Wilson arrived at his house about 5:30 A.M. asking for a drink of water. His description of the murder scene supported Martin's: "The culvert is in a hollow, there is some brush nearby. The grass was about one and a half feet high in the culvert."

James Martin made neat pencil diagrams of the road, the slough, the culvert and the car, from two vantage points. They are elegant, detailed drawings, and the report includes the beautifully handwritten notes of Sergeant Drysdale.

Next they interviewed John Neufeldt, who recounted his memories of that morning in detail, going over much the same story as Isaac with one or two additions: "He also had a new shovel with him. He gave it to me when I drove him to Blaine Lake. I have it now. He said he carried it because he sometimes got in the sand . . . Under the culvert there was some dirt and the man shovelled some of this onto the car. He looked pretty sick and white. He vomited in my yard . . . He did not talk very much on the way up to Blaine Lake. He borrowed a topcoat from me for the ride."

John Neufeldt produced the shovel with the Ashdown Hardware label still on it.

Henry Williams confirmed the absence of geese in the burning car, and told them Isaac Peters had taken a picture of the car later that day. The police returned to Saskatoon with photos of the burned car, to the delight of the newspaper reporters.

Drysdale was at first skeptical that a car leaving the grade at that point would land on its wheels. "It seems to me that the chances of one car in a hundred performing the same feat again would be very slight indeed." But after a thorough examination of the area, Drysdale concluded his report to Inspector Prime with the following observations:

Before leaving we felt satisfied that there was nothing in that place which caused the search, . . . and in view of the other circumstances which had become known to us beforehand . . . the zigzag tracks leading over the grade, his extreme nervousness and nausea . . . these considerations led us to believe that he must have arrived at that spot shortly before and that he actually had the accident . . . Unless something is learned in the meantime it would appear that a house to house search is necessary throughout the district between Saskatoon and the scene of the accident, for obvious reasons . . .

From the facts contained in this report there is every indication that Wilson buried the body some place before the accident to the car happened.

John Wilson had done a good job of drawing attention away from the culvert. By now, members of the Military Police, the Royal North West Mounted Police, and the Saskatchewan Provincial Police had walked over, around and *through* the culvert, right over Polly Wilson's shallow grave. A few days after their joint patrol, Sergeant Sparkman returned to the site and took four snapshots, including one of himself standing by the culvert to show the approximate height of the culvert which he measured at four feet six inches, its width at six feet four inches.

∽

The Saskatoon *Daily Star*, November 14, 1919:

TRIAL TO BE HELD IN SASKATOON
A mystery so baffling and a crime so dastardly that its only parallel in

modern criminal annals is the famous Dr. Crippen case is now being investigated by provincial police . . .

Police think the body of Mrs. Wilson was either burned in the car or thrown in a slough.

Sergt. Wilson was brought back under escort from Vancouver when relatives of his former wife wrote that the woman had not been heard from for 14 months . . . while they pleaded with the authorities to ascertain why their daughter did not write, she was lying dead in an unnamed grave, while her former husband deceived a trusting girl, whom he married within a few hours of his first wife's death.

The large eastern dailies also jumped on the story. "BELIEVE MAN DID AWAY WITH FIRST WIFE TO MARRY SECOND," shrilled the Montreal *Daily Star*, "MURDER SUSPECT TRIED TO END LIFE."

The Saskatoon *Daily Star* posed these questions:

— Did Sergeant Wilson, RNWMP, burn the body of his first wife, Mary "Polly" Wilson, when he destroyed the automobile, or did he kill the woman and later burn the car to obliterate traces of the murder? Or did he kill her at all? . . .
— Sergt. Wilson came back to Saskatoon without his overcoat. Did he burn the overcoat because there were blood stains on the garment?
— The hunt for the woman's body is gradually narrowing down.
— Residents of district urged to be on lookout for unidentified grave.

The newspaper accounts encouraged avid readers to try to solve the mystery, and armchair detectives abounded. Some went further. Armed with shovels, they combed the countryside around Blaine Lake and Waldheim and points along the road between there and Saskatoon, looking for the grave of that poor soul who came all the way from Scotland.

People couldn't get enough of it.

On November 17, the Saskatoon *Daily Star* published a photograph of Polly Wilson and her two children. Polly's abundant shining hair was piled up in the style of the time, and a slight smile pulled at her lips. Her large, clear eyes, and those of the children, were intently fixed on a spot somewhere to the right. Below this picture was the picture of the burned Grey Dort. The next day the *Star* added another human interest element:

> Jessie Patterson, whom Wilson married the day after the disappearance of his first wife, is at Blaine Lake, Sask. She will become a mother about the end of this year and in the meantime the authorities are not questioning her. She is believed to be entirely innocent of any knowledge of the alleged murder and police are humanely leaving her to herself until Wilson's child is born. Questioning at this stage might seriously affect her health.

In fact, at this time, Jessie was barely four months pregnant.

Chapter XXXVII
BLOOD-STAINED LOVE LETTERS

Before Jessie went home to Blaine Lake, the police had confiscated the Wilsons' two trunks and left them in the room where Jack and Jessie had stayed. The unlocked trunk held only clothes and a few household items. The other was locked and its key lost or taken home by Jessie. At the Grand Hotel, Provincial Police Assistant Superintendent William Tracey, a tall, lean Scot with a sharp mind and dour sense of humour, watched as Sergeant Corby tried and discarded key after key, finally shaking his head and standing up.

"It's no go with any of these, sir."

"All right, sergeant. Round up some more keys, and if we have to, we'll break the lock."

Constable Scotney, in a room at the Blaine Lake Hotel, stood up as Jessie entered the room gripping her father's arm. She appeared unwell and pale, but she walked erect and looked Constable Scotney in the eye. He pulled out a chair for her.

"Please sit down, Mrs. Wilson. You, too, Mr. Patterson."

They sat, with Scotney at a small table facing them.

"I realize this is very difficult for you, ma'am. It won't take long."

"That's good. Jessie is in a very . . . She can't take much more right now," John Patterson said.

"I understand. I mainly wanted to ask you, Mrs. Wilson, if you know where we might locate your husband's shotgun."

She shook her head. "I don't know where it is. He lent it to an inspector in Vancouver to go duck shooting."

"When was that? Do you remember?"

"Just this fall sometime."

"And do you know his name?"

"No. I don't." There was a trace of anger in her voice. At what, or whom, Constable Scotney could not tell. Perhaps just at circumstances.

"Thank you, Mrs. Wilson. I appreciate your coming down."

John Patterson stayed behind a moment.

"Jessie will answer questions later. It's just that she's very delicate right now. Her mother or I have to be with her all the time."

⌒

Conrad Read's statement arrived on Commissioner Perry's desk. It was startling in its revelation that Wilson had told him that he and Jessie would be married on the evening of September 27. Read recounted the episode of the missing Colt pistol which he later found in Wilson's desk, and then the shotgun:

I first saw the 12 gauge shotgun in the office of John Wilson in the Armory in Saskatoon. Wilson invariably took the shotgun with him when making a trip into the country with his car, and it kicked around in the bottom of the car about as much as it did in the office, or rather in the bottom of the car that was burned, and also the car that replaced the one which was burned. [Read describes cleaning the gun when it was left at his place.] I am satisfied I should know the gun again [detailed description here] . . . The maker was Parker of Edinburgh.

I knew nothing of Wilson's home affairs, but believed from remarks he had made from time to time that his mother and father were both dead, that he had lost a sister in France during the War, and not very long ago had lost his only other sister who died in Scotland, that he had a brother in England who had been made prisoner by the Germans but had escaped in the fall of 1918 and who stood small chance of recovery from his wounds.

Read's statement points up Wilson's tendency to lie when he wanted something and to fabricate stories about his "tragic" siblings, who were in reality all alive and well back in Scotland and had not heard a word from Jack since 1914.

Wilson, still at the police hospital, improved daily, and police planned to move him to the Regina jail at the end of the week.

Men from the SPP combed through the rubbish at the Cory Nuisance Ground for the remains of the burned car. The newspapers duly reported: "The rubbish heaps in Cory Nuisance Ground yielded broken, flame-scarred parts which were identified as belonging to Wilson's car. But what the police were really looking for—the portion of the tonneau wall which a bullet is believed to have penetrated— had not been discovered at press time."

And an SPP constable spent day after day showing Wilson's photograph at every hardware and general store in Wilson's large territory in the hopes that a clerk would say, "I know that man. He bought a shovel here."

✺

Back at the Grand Hotel, the seventh key was tried and—*click*—it worked. Sergeant Corby smiled up at Assistant Superintendent Tracey.

"Lucky seven," he said and, lifting the lid, carefully opened Wilson's trunk all the way back.

On the left side of the tray lay a brown leather dispatch bag, filthy, scorched, and covered with blood.

"Good God," breathed Bill Tracey, as he hunkered his long frame down for a closer look. "Does that look like blood to you, Corby?"

"I would say so, sir." They looked at each other and smiled.

"Well, let's have a look inside."

Carefully he undid the straps and lifted the flap. Tracey whistled at the sight. Thick, crusted blood had stuck the scorched flap and straps to the case. The marks showing that the bag had been opened long after the blood dried were clearly visible in a thick, dark outline.

"I think we just may have our murder witness, Sergeant," he said. "You'd better take notes as I examine the contents."

"Yes, sir." Sergeant Corby produced notebook and pen, and pulled a chair up to the open trunk.

Tracey reached for a large blue envelope in the inside pocket of the case. It had been stuck to the leather at one time, the front of the envelope and its contents liberally stained with what appeared to be blood. Tracey drew out the contents, all Military Police papers: a copy of the Military Service Act, 1917, a quantity of forms used in enforcing it, copies of reports submitted by Wilson, circular descriptions of persons wanted under the MSA, and other papers. As he looked at each paper, he identified it to Sergeant Corby, who listed it.

Tracey then opened another pocket in the bag, also stained inside, and spread the contents of a large, bulky envelope out on the hotel room floor. They were obviously personal letters, most of them addressed to Jessie Patterson in Blaine Lake and Prince Albert, and some addressed from Jessie to Wilson in Regina, Saskatoon and other places. Tracey pulled out the letters and laid them down on their envelopes. "My Dearest Jessie," "Dearest Wee Girl," "My Darling Jessie," there were a lot of them, some in Wilson's handwriting, some typed on an office typewriter. Most were from Wilson to Jessie, with hers to him much more restrained in salutation—"Dear Jack" or once "Dearest Jack."

"A quantity of personal letters," Tracey dictated, his voice barely able to contain his excitement, "from Jack Wilson to Jessie Patterson and vice versa, covering a period from"—he scanned the letters— "the early part of 1917 until the date of their marriage in late September 1918."

Many of the letters were also stained with the same substance, which had at some time oozed into the openings of the case and onto the papers.

"We'll submit these to Dr. Charlton tomorrow." C. M. Charlton was the coroner and provincial analyst. "If it's human blood, Wilson's going to have to think of something besides a cut finger."

"Should I say let's hope it is?"

"Might as well say it as think it," said Tracey. "And I'd lay money on whose it is."

"No takers," Sergeant Corby said. "But why would he hang on to it?"

"That's what I'd like to know." Tracey lifted the tray and saw a quantity of ladies' clothes, blankets, a coffee pot and other household articles, all neatly packed. He felt through them without disturbing the neat contents too much. "His wife must have seen it; it looks as if she packed the trunk. How the devil would he explain the condition of the case? Anybody would think it was blood."

"He must have concocted some story, sir."

"Yes, Wilson is quick with a story, I gather. And it was duck hunting time."

"He might have said he'd thrown some ducks or geese on top of it."

"Possibly. And it seems as if she believed everything he said—both before and after they were married."

Tracey began returning the letters to their envelopes. "I'll read these at the office." He glanced at the letter he'd just picked up.

"Listen to this, Sergeant. 'I am almost a free man now, Dearest, just a few more days. I may have been married and had to get a divorce but, thank God, even if I am no Christian I can look back on a miserable life and say I never harmed a miserable girl in my life.' "

"What an honourable man, our Sergeant Wilson. And look at the way he signs his letters. 'Your honest, faithful and true, Jack boy.' " Tracey picked up one after another, his voice incredulous and amused. " 'Your loving, kind and true Jack Boy.' And listen to this one, 'Your honest, clean and true, Jack.' "

At this, both men burst out laughing.

"*Clean*, too? Well, how could she resist him?" Tracey said.

"How could she believe him, you mean?"

"Well, she was young, wasn't she? Very young and very gullible. Poor girl."

"Poor first wife, I say."

"Yes, indeed. Both of them."

Tracey was scanning through some of the letters.

"Well, we've got him by the short hairs, I think, with these. He talks about marrying this girl in just about every letter, most of them written before his wife conveniently died."

He gathered up the letters, carefully replacing them in their corresponding envelopes. "Charles Augustus will be most interested to read these," he said with a delighted grin.

"These last two are letters to Jessie from someone else. This one signed, 'Your dying sister, Mary.' Good heavens! And one from some minister in the old country. I'll have a look at them later." Tracey returned the papers to the case.

"Shall I list the other things in the trunk now?"

"I don't think we need to now. You can do that later. There aren't any more papers or any photographs that I could see."

Sergeant Corby locked the trunk again before leaving the hotel room.

Back in his office, Bill Tracey read Wilson's two forged letters to Jessie. In the one signed "Your dying sister, Mary," the signature was so shaky it was difficult to read.

Tracey shook his head several times while reading the letter. Little did Wilson know when making references to the Glasgow Holiday and other details that the letter would be read by a sharp-minded Scot with six years' experience with the Burg of Partick Police in Scotland. After reading "the minister's" letter to Jessie, he sat deep in thought for a time, then scrawled a few lines on a page and tossed the letters into his In tray. He rolled a legal-size sheet of paper into his typewriter and began his report to the commissioner:

It will be seen that the above letters cover a period commencing in the early part of 1917 until the date of the marriage in 1918 . . . but I notice that in the letters dated May 1918 Wilson apparently becomes madly infatuated with Miss Patterson and declares that it is impossible for him to live without her . . . I also draw your attention to the fact that Mary Wilson arrived in Saskatoon in April of 1918, and immediately Wilson redoubles his efforts to gain the hand of Jessie Patterson . . .

I also found two typewritten letters alleged to be written from the

Royal Infirmary, Glasgow, Scotland. One of these letters . . . is supposed to be written by Wilson's sister, who at the time of writing is supposed to be dying . . . the writer then goes on to tell Jessie about her brother John's previous marriage . . . making particular reference to the unfaithfulness of his first wife and ends by commending Jessie to his care and hopes that they will be happy together. This appears to be a rather peculiar statement for a dying girl to make as she apparently gives her sanction to her beloved brother committing the crime of bigamy. You will also note that speaking of the wedding preparations, she states that they cost John several thousand dollars. In my experience it is very rarely that old country people speak of dollars when speaking of money, they always refer to pounds . . .

The second letter . . . evidently a minister who also appears to be in the possession of the particulars regarding the previous marriage of Wilson and his unhappy marriage with his first wife . . . This writer also commends Miss Patterson to the care of Wilson and prays for their future happiness. He also gives his sanction to the crime of bigamy being committed which, to say the least, is a most unusual thing for a Minister of the Gospel to do . . . There is no mention of Wilson having obtained a divorce from his first wife . . . Old Country divorces are much more easily obtained than in Canada and if as stated Mary Wilson was of an immoral character I am of the opinion that it would have been an easy matter for him to have obtained a Decree of Divorce. That this was not done is evident by Mrs. Wilson's arrival in Regina in April, 1918 . . .

Another point which strikes me as peculiar is the reference to Wilson meeting Mary Hutchison during the Glasgow Holiday and marrying her ten months later. To my own knowledge the pleasure boats on the river Clyde do not commence until the beginning of June and what is known as the Glasgow Fair Holidays are an annual event always held from the 10th to the 20th of July, which would put the date of his wedding sometime between March or April 1908. Since he was married on New Year's Day, 1908, I am of the opinion that the story told in this letter was a false one.

✎

In a joint patrol on November 21, Sergeant Drysdale and SPP officers Inspector Smith and Sergeant Sparkman drove to Blaine Lake to interview the threshermen once more. As Inspector Smith had not seen the site of the burned car, they drove first to the culvert. The zigzag tracks made by Wilson's car were still visible. The three examined the bushes around the site and those on the way to Isaac Neufeldt's, where Wilson had gone for water that morning. A filled-in hole covered with broken branches caused some excitement, but they dug down to sand and clay without result. They again examined the well in the slough.

Then, calling at first one farm and then another, they talked to the men who had been there that day.

They found Henry Funk out in his shop, oiling a piece of machinery secured in a vice. He waved them to sit wherever they could and carried on with his work.

"We were first at the machine that morning, Isaac Peters and I. I was running the machine, eh? and it was dark yet, around five o'clock. I heard a car going north, travelling real fast with no lights. That would be before six o'clock. Then I saw a big smoke go up." Henry waved the oilcan, spraying oil in all directions. "A big white smoke, and after that a black smoke." A few more drops flew up. "By then the other boys were there and I said, 'That's gasoline burning. Let's go down and have a look.' "

When Smith asked Henry about Wilson's actions at the car, he laughed.

"That guy was drunk. He'd been sick everywhere. And he was acting kind of queer."

"In what way?"

"Oh, he told different fellows different stories about how the car got there, eh? And he kept going back and forth, getting dirt from under the culvert and throwing it on the car. I guess he was doing it just to be doing something but he seemed in a daze."

Next they went to see Isaac Peters. They sat around the kitchen table, and Mrs. Peters poured them coffee. Then she discreetly withdrew to another part of the house.

Peters told them the same story about seeing a car and then smoke. "It was just getting light and I could see one person in it, and then we saw the smoke. Some of the boys got on the elevator to look."

"The elevator?" Sergeant Sparkman asked.

"Yeah, you know, on the threshing machine? And they saw a big car burning. And there was no car down there when Henry and I passed over the culvert going to work."

When asked about Wilson, Peters laughed. "That man wasn't sober. He looked like he'd been dragged through a knothole backwards. And he told some funny stories, too, you know, that he had geese in the car that burned and so forth, but we would have smelled them. I figured he concocted a story about the car catching fire before he went over the grade in case somebody asked us. It was a police car he burned up, and he was driving awful darned fast with no lights."

At John Neufeldt's farm they talked to John and to Agnes Neufeldt, "seventeen years old next March," who had been in the back seat when her father drove Wilson to Blaine Lake. Drysdale asked if she remembered the drive.

"Oh, yes. The four of us were in the back seat. There was a yellow straw valise on the floor with bright red spatters on it. I asked the man Wilson if it was blood and he took it in the front with him and said it was from the geese."

"Did he say anything else?"

"I don't think so. He seemed kind of mad that we asked."

John Neufeldt also remembered Wilson being annoyed that the children had noticed the spots. He again told about Wilson borrowing his coat for the ride and giving him the shovel that he "had no more use for" when he got out at Blaine Lake.

They also talked to Nicholas Boldt, another of the threshers.

Detective Sergeant Sparkman, SPP, commented in his report:

It will be particularly noticed that Nicholas Boldt says that Wilson had an overcoat on, he thinks a slicker of "a light colour." This latter should be noted as subsequent investigation showed that Wilson was supposed to have burned his coat, according to his own statement, and that he borrowed a dark coat from John Neufeldt to go to Blaine Lake . . . The question remains when did he do away with this coat.

Sparkman concludes his report on the patrol:

From the above it appears established as a fact that Wilson arrived at the spot where the car was burned at about 5:30 A.M. and that the fire was simultaneous. It would now seem certain that the fire was the direct result of the car going over the grade and that the going over was an accident . . . From all these circumstances it now appears clear that Wilson would have had no time to do much or any digging in the vicinity where the car burned, and it necessarily follows that the body of Mrs. Wilson is not in the immediate vicinity . . . This is now beyond conjecture.

It will also be noted that apparently Wilson was travelling without headlights although the time was too dark to do so. This may be that he was wishing to attract as little attention as possible along the road. This also strengthens the theory that the accident and burning was not intentional. Also the story that Wilson filled the car at Saskatoon early in the morning cannot be substantiated, and was no doubt only said to establish the story that he was at Saskatoon over night of the 27th when he was no doubt in the country at some point disposing of his first wife.

Chapter xxxviii
∾ NEW PLAYERS ∾

One by one Jack Wilson encountered the new players in the drama he had set in motion that night by the culvert.

Superintendent Bill Tracey visited him at the Mounted Police hospital and pulled out the two forged letters to Jessie. Tracey told him the reasons he knew they were forged, and that he'd already sent them to the Stirlingshire police for confirmation.

"Do you admit that you forged these letters, Jack?"

"Yes."

"For what purpose?"

He refused to answer that. He wasn't going to tell them anything they didn't already know. Especially where he'd put Polly.

The next day Tracey and Inspector Smith took him out of the hospital to SPP headquarters and into the office of Inspector Goldsmith. Goldsmith was a small man with a moustache and round, gold-rimmed glasses. Wilson had heard of him: he was a Boer War veteran and reputed to be sharp as they come.

Wilson stood in front of Goldsmith's desk. Tracey was seated to the left of Goldsmith; Smith stood against the wall behind him. Facing them all like that, Jack felt his legs go weak and shaky. Then he noticed the large manila envelope on Goldsmith's desk and recognized it as one from Jessie's trunk.

Goldsmith just looked at him for some time. The inspector's beady eyes looked right through him, and his right eyebrow soared up as if he wouldn't believe a word anybody said.

Finally he spoke. "Has your memory improved regarding what happened to your wife, Mary Wilson?"

"No. I don't know what happened to her."

"Why don't you know?"

"My mind is in a haze."

"Surely you remember that she died?"

"No. Yes. I remember she died but I don't know how."

Goldsmith picked up the envelope and emptied its contents on his desk: photographs of Jack and Jessie in Blaine Lake and Prince Albert, Jessie in her nurse's uniform, Jessie in her new car, Jessie and him separately on the trip west, the two of them with Con and Nell, Jessie and Nell laughing on the beach at English Bay.

Goldsmith dropped the photograph of Polly and the two children on top of the pile.

"Is this a photograph of your first wife, Mary Wilson?"

"Yes."

"Where did you bury her body?"

He didn't answer.

"We've got all day, Wilson."

"I can't remember."

"Do you remember where she died?" Tracey asked.

"No. Somewhere on the way to Blaine Lake."

"How close to Blaine Lake?"

"I don't know. I don't know how it happened or where it happened. I wrote it all in my statement, and that's all I know."

"Are those your children with your wife in the photograph?" Goldsmith asked.

"Yes."

"For their sake, don't you think you should tell where their mother is buried?" Inspector Smith said.

Silence. Outside the window on Goldsmith's right, dry snowflakes eddied and swirled from a leaden sky. A sudden gust of wind rattled the window; a cold, mournful sound.

"What about the rest of her family, Jack?" Tracey asked. "Her mother and father are ill now, and this terrible thing is making it harder for them. At least let them arrange a decent burial for their daughter."

He just clamped his lips together. They'd never make him tell. As long as they didn't have a body, they couldn't charge him with murder.

"Think of the mother of your children, Wilson. Lying out in cold ground in some lonely place."

He just shook his head. Good Lord, he thought, what kind of awful story were they going to come up with next?

Then they changed tactics.

"Did you know Jessie is ill?" Tracey asked.

"No!" He felt the colour drain from his face.

"She is very ill. This is all very hard on her, you know."

Tears sprang into his eyes, he couldn't help it.

"She didn't lose the baby, did she?" He steadied himself with the edge of the desk.

"No, she hasn't lost the baby. But she could if this goes on much longer."

"The doctors are worried about her condition. She is very, *very* ill," Goldsmith said.

He couldn't stand it any longer. "I won't tell you anything more until you let me see Jessie."

"Then you do remember where you buried your wife?" Goldsmith said.

"I won't say anything about it till I see Jessie. I need to tell her myself."

Goldsmith leaned back in his chair and looked at Wilson—impaled him, it felt like—with his small piercing eyes. He made a pyramid with his short fingers. "Well, Mr. Wilson, I can't see that talking to you is going to make her feel any better. I understand you are being transferred to the Regina jail. We will bring you here two hours each day until your memory returns. Now good day to you." He began to gather up the snapshots from his desk.

Jack wanted to ask for one of the pictures of Jessie, but he didn't.

He could hardly walk down the corridor. His legs felt like rubber, and perspiration slid down his ribs. Tracey opened the outside door and motioned him through. As the cold wind hit him, he shook like a leaf from head to foot.

On their way to the car, they met Superintendent Mahony. He was dressed in plainclothes, a handsome bald man with even features and intelligent eyes. A man you would notice anywhere.

Mahony looked Wilson over, then he and Tracey walked away a few paces and talked in low voices for a few minutes. Once, at something Tracey said, Mahony flashed a smile, and Jack could see why his men were so fond of him. Why hadn't things worked out for *him*? He could have been a superintendent himself some day.

He felt relieved to be back in his jail cell. It was peaceful, and it was warm.

∽

That evening, Tracey, Smith and Goldsmith fielded various theories regarding where and how Wilson had hidden his wife's body. They were in Tracey's office, drinking coffee, all relaxed in chairs now. An ashtray on the desk was slowly filling with cigarette and cigar ashes.

"He could have buried her anywhere between Saskatoon and Blaine Lake," Tracey said. "Or maybe he just said that to put us off. It could be past Blaine Lake, or God knows where."

"Like looking for a needle in a haystack," Smith agreed.

"Say! Do you suppose he might have put the body in a haystack and set fire to it?"

"It's possible. He wouldn't be the first to do that," Goldsmith said.

"And there'd be lots of them around, after harvest," Tracey said.

"I could go up there and ask around if there were any suspicious or malicious fires around that time," Smith offered.

"Good idea," Tracey agreed. "When can you leave?"

"Tomorrow morning?" Smith said, without much hope.

Tracey grinned. "Tonight."

Smith glanced at the clock on the wall. "Yes, sir. I'll catch the late train."

Smith and Goldsmith left Tracey's office, and as they walked down the hall, they heard typewriter keys clattering behind Tracey's door. They looked at each other and shook their heads, it was eleven o'clock.

In his report to Mahony, Tracey wrote:

I am of the opinion that Wilson has made up his mind that unless the Police are successful in locating the body . . . they will not be in a position to place a charge of murder against him.

The accused appears to feel his position very deeply and when mention is made of Jessie Patterson he appears to be on the verge of a breakdown . . . when the name of Polly Wilson and her people is mentioned the accused does not appear to take it to heart and shows an utter disregard for any of his own or Polly Wilson's relatives in Scotland . . . I am of the opinion that if the accused will ever divulge the secret of where Polly Wilson's body is to be found, it will be through Jessie Patterson or her people.

But Tracey also knew that Jessie might not be in a hurry to see her husband charged with murder—especially if he had told her after he was arrested that it was an accident. "I trust you, husband," she had said, when she came to see him in the guardroom.

And if Jessie's family did not pressure Jack to tell the truth and get it over with, what then?

Chapter xxxix

✍ A SOULLESS SCOUNDREL ✍

When the second cable came, telling them Polly had died at Wilson's hands the previous November, Elizabeth and Archie Craig went back to Slamannan to break the news. Since Polly's mother had been so upset at the news of Wilson's remarriage, they decided to show the cable to Elizabeth's father first. William Hutchison was shocked at the accusation, but not surprised to know that Polly was dead. He already knew it in his heart.

"But I can't believe that Jack took Polly's life. He's been false and untruthful, but never would he do such a thing to Polly. I won't believe that of him."

"Oh, I pray God you are right, Father, and Polly died a natural death," said Elizabeth. "Maybe she died in an accident?"

Archie shook his head. "I think we should prepare for the worst. The police have as much as said so, haven't they?"

"But what will we say to Mother?" Elizabeth cried. "It would kill her to think that Polly's life may have been taken from her."

"We have to tell her we've lost Polly," William said. "But not what they suspect."

"But it will be in all the newspapers. How can we keep it from her?"

"We must try to keep it out of the papers. Everyone around here knows the family," Archie said.

"Oh, God, what did he do with her if he harmed her? Did he give her a decent burial, I wonder?" This had been on Elizabeth's mind since the cable arrived. "Perhaps she's not really gone. I dreamed I saw her sitting with a baby in long clothes on her knees in a bare log cabin, and Jack entered a long passage. As soon as he came near, Polly wept bitterly." Elizabeth wept as she told it. "I asked her what was wrong and she said something about bread. That dream left such a vivid impression it worried me for weeks. Like a warning I could do nothing about. Do you think he might have put her in some out-of-the-way place?"

"I doubt that, Lizzie," William said gently. "I think we must accept that we've lost Polly."

"But if he married in September, and the cable said she died in November, where was she for those two months? You know how she would grieve at his abandoning her in a strange land. She must have spent two sore months somewhere."

William Hutchison shook his head. "I'll never understand how he could forget those bairns. Any father would be proud of them."

"And their beautiful house," Elizabeth said. "Just the way she left it." She didn't wipe away the tears that ran down her cheeks. They had almost become natural to her.

Her father just shook his head. "I ought to write to the commissioner. But I've tried more than once and I cannot."

"Nor can I," said Elizabeth.

"James will reply, I'm sure," Archie said.

And Polly's brother did, on December 10, conveying the family's gratitude to the commissioner for his handling of the case. Unlike his sister Elizabeth, James Hutchison was nothing if not direct. At the end of his short letter he wrote: "My intimate relations with Wilson date from March 1909, and I found him out to be a liar, a rogue, and a soulless scoundrel."

Commissioner Perry had advised the family on December 8 that Polly's body had not yet been found but that the police were sparing no efforts in trying to locate it. His letters to the family were unfailingly kind and sympathetic.

Elizabeth wrote again, detailing Jack's treatment of Polly:

She loved him and could see no wrong in him and it was not for us to wound her by showing her his falseness . . .

As a girl she was like a wee fairy, she was so thin with a mass of long golden curls. She was always brave and would have laughed at what would have made me weep and it seems she needed all her bravery. She told a teacher friend that she would lay down her life for her husband if it would let him get on in the world . . .

She always thought he would come back and take his place in the nursery again for he left a beautiful home here. It is still as my sister left it . . . Oh, isn't it all so very sad? Now in finishing I hope again he is not guilty. It makes me so sad to think that the children's father is in prison.

∾

They wouldn't let him rest; they hounded and hounded him. No sooner were the Provincial Police finished than the Mounties came at him.

"What did you do with your shotgun?" they asked.

"I sold it in Vancouver."

"When was that?"

"About six weeks ago."

"To whom did you sell it?"

"I don't know his name."

"Where does he live?"

"I don't know. I was never at his home."

"Where did you meet him?"

"I don't remember."

And then Tracey and Goldsmith had another round with him about the dispatch case.

"Did you hide the case from your wife, Jessie?"

"No."

"Then how did you explain the presence of so much blood on it?"

"I told her it was oil."

"Wasn't she suspicious?"

"No. She trusted me."

Goldsmith cast his eyes to the ceiling.

They wanted to know about the car: how it caught fire, what caused the accident, where he was going, and on and on.

What didn't they want to know about? That's what he'd like to know. He was afraid to open his eyes in the morning, in case there'd be a policeman standing by his bed.

∾

From the wording before and after the crossed-out words in Wilson's statement, it was thought the hidden words were a reference to the burial site. The provincial police tried everything to decipher them. They first photographed the document, hoping this might enlarge the erasure (it didn't) and also in case the original document became damaged by tests. They took the original document to Dr. Manning, a chemistry expert at the university in Saskatoon, to see if the iodine vapour test would work. Dr. Manning held out no hope for separating the original words from the applied lead of the crossing out, both consisting of the same material. They subjected the original to much magnifying and microscopic testing. They lifted a considerable portion of the erasing pencil with candle grease, heat and friction, but still they couldn't read the underlying words. They X-rayed it. They even had it projected onto the screen at a motion picture house.

The words kept their secret.

On December 8, 1919, a letter for John Wilson was forwarded to Charles Mahony. On December 10, Superintendent Mahony had the letter delivered to John Wilson. The next day there was a break in the case.

Chapter XL

✒ FATE SEEMED TO GO AGAINST ME ✒

On December 11, Bill Tracey received a phone call from the Regina jail. Wilson wanted to make another statement. Tracey didn't give him time to change his mind.

When Tracey arrived at the jail, Wilson told his story. He had met Polly's train, and they had stopped at Cairns Store before heading out into the country and stopping to shoot some geese. He said that after he had shot some geese and returned to the car:

> she [Polly] went over to the right hand side of the car and got in her seat again. I went and looked at the radiator, then I came back to my own side of the car . . .
>
> I was just opening the door to go into the car, when my right foot slipped and I remember her saying "Watch J . . ." I think it was "Jack"

she was going to say; that was just when I was putting my right hand up
to catch the side of the car, that was the hand I had the gun in, when the
gun went off. I remember I shouted something, "My God, Polly." I saw
that she was hit in the head, here (pointing to the right temple); I don't
remember exactly what I done and I went over to the left side, put my
arm around her and shouted and shouted, then I ran around and
jumped in the car and started the car up and after it was going I steered
with the left hand and had my right arm around her, holding her . . .
shouting to her all the time . . . and I knew she was dead anyway.

Wilson told about driving wildly to within sight of Saskatoon, then
deciding to turn around and go to Dr. Langlois at Marcelin. The lights
burned out on the way, and the car jumped the grade.

When the car landed, with the jolt of the car hitting the ground, she fell;
I was still holding her, but she fell out of the door of the right hand
car . . . I went clean off my head altogether, then I don't know how long
I was around there nor anything nor what I was doing. The first thing I
remember clear after that I was sitting in the grass beside her, she was
lying on her back on the grass and her feet were on the running-board of
the car.

I sat there thinking for a while, wondering what I could do now, then I
figured out that nobody would ever believe this story I told, that it was
an accident or anything else, so I went in the back of the car and I got a
shovel. I dug her a grave under the culvert.

It was getting daylight then and there was a car passed overhead with
threshermen in it, and they passed over when I was still working, then I
went back and looked at the car and there was quite a bit of blood in the
front seat and I . . . took the satchel . . . out and set fire in the front seat
of the car . . . and quite a few threshers came down . . . and while I was
going into Blaine Lake in the car and all day Saturday I thought about
going away, but I did not. Jessie and I were married on Sunday night at
Saskatoon.

It seemed funny. Everything—fate seemed to go against me all the
time. After the first time when she came from the Old Country. I did not
know she was coming here. I was in Prince Albert one day, trying to

enlist in the Mounted Police Overseas Draft, and was talking to the Superintendent (Routledge) and when she phoned him from Regina asking him where I was, that was the first time I had been in that office for nearly a year and if I had not been there that day, he would have sent her to Blaine Lake to me.

And then again that night when we were going to Blaine Lake and I would tell Jessie everything. She knew all about Jessie and then the accident happened and even then, my intentions were good . . .

Just about two or three weeks before I left Vancouver, I took the gun down to a second hand store on Cordova Street, Vancouver . . . When you leave the CPR you come on to Cordova then you swing to the left and come to a bunch of second hand stores, . . . all the second-hand stores are bunched together in there. I think it is a Jewish woman that was in there. She will have it on her returns. I gave my right name to her . . .

The suitcase that Mrs. Wilson had was just a cheap wicker suitcase and did not wear no time. I have her rings. I was intending to keep them for the little boy. I think I have them in the trunks. They were just two rings, one marriage ring and there is a diamond in the engagement ring. I think she would have her purse with her. I did not look to see if she had. I put the robe of the car around the body. I put the body into the culvert from the right hand side. It is not buried very deep, the head was put in first from that side next to the car.

This is all I have to say. There is nothing else, the only thing that I wish to state is that this statement is made voluntarily and no inducements or promises have been held out to me for same. This statement is made to Assistant Superintendent Tracey of the Saskatchewan Provincial Police, Regina.

The letter Wilson received on December 10 had apparently changed his mind. If the police were right, it was from Jessie or Jessie's family on her behalf. In any case, the wait was finally over.

He described Polly's suitcase as "just a cheap wicker suitcase and did not wear no time." Polly must have given him the expensive leather suitcase, her farewell gift from Elizabeth and Archie. Or he borrowed it when he left for Saskatoon. She probably thought the handsome leather case more appropriate to his position than hers.

∾

On the evening of December 11, Sergeant Drysdale received a call from SPP Inspector Smith that Wilson had told them where he'd buried the body. Bright and early on December 12, Smith, Drysdale and Sparkman drove to the culvert, armed with picks, axes and shovels. With two local men from the district, and a team of horses with stoneboat standing by, they began to dig in the frozen ground.

About a foot down they came to a pair of ladies boots set at a 45-degree angle. The boots had bones in them and decomposed flesh. They worked until dark, then continued the following morning.

The body was buried about four feet deep at the hips. Clothing was pulled up over the knees, and the torso and head wrapped in a coarse blanket. The body appeared to have been thrown in the oddly shaped grave, with no care taken to straighten the limbs. The body was removed along with much frozen soil. After photographs were taken of the body from all angles, and of the excavation, Coroner C. M. Charlton ordered the body removed to Saskatoon.

The news that the body had been found in the culvert must have come as a shock to both police forces, since the investigators had so thoroughly ruled out the culvert as a burial site. The avid followers of the case must have pounced on that, and the fact that it was right beside the car.

To many, it seemed incomprehensible that the investigators had consistently turned a blind eye to the culvert. Their conviction, however, was based on the two statements that the grass was about one and a half feet high in the culvert the day the car burned, and on Drysdale's unequivocal assertion: "The ground under the culvert was, after the fire, known to be covered with growing grass and weeds, and she cannot be buried there." And Detective Sergeant Sparkman, SPP, had concluded that the accident had just happened, giving Wilson no time to do any digging in that vicinity: "This is now beyond conjecture," Sparkman had concluded in his report.

Before beginning to dig Polly's grave, Wilson must have sliced off the top layer of soil, including plant roots, and returned it when he was finished. The following summer, the grasses and weeds grew again. Still, if the culvert was overgrown with grass and weeds, how did they account for the loose dirt he took from under the culvert to throw on the car?

Detective Sergeant Drysdale was one of many who gave a lot of thought to the chronology of events the day of the murder and the reason they hadn't suspected the body was right there. His report to Commissioner Perry dealing with the recovery of the body, the postmortem and inquest, ended with these comments:

> A perusal again of the statements taken in this case shows in the main that several persons arrived at car within 10 or 15 minutes of the time the smoke was seen, and taking into consideration that two people saw a car going North and saw the smoke shortly afterwards, I cannot understand how Wilson could have been at the culvert as long as he states he was (I have read his last statement) and above all, to have time to remove traces so well. I am strongly of the opinion now that the body was recovered from under the culvert, that at the time of the accident, it was his second appearance at that place. [Actually, it was his third appearance. On the first, he killed Polly. On the second, he buried her. And on the last, he accidentally went over the bank while fleeing the scene.] . . .
>
> The evidence as to the using of the shovel by Wilson at the car suggested and was understood as if he were merely throwing on a little dirt haphazardly, like the futile action of any other man, having come over the grade as he had done.

The other question, the most puzzling of all, is, why did Wilson, after leaving the site, drive off the road exactly there, almost pointing to the grave? He was driving fast with no lights on, as if trying not to be seen, and probably on his way to Blaine Lake. The police eventually concluded that he went over at the spot accidentally. An uncanny coincidence?

∽

On the morning of December 15, Dr. Charlton held the post-mortem. Tracey and Goldsmith picked up Wilson and drove downtown. Wilson wondered why they didn't tell him where they were going, but he didn't give them the satisfaction of asking.

At a building he didn't recognize, they went in and down some stairs. The heavy door whooshed open and the smell of formaldehyde and decay hit him. He saw several large steel cabinets, a large sink and long, enamel-topped cupboards. And on a table in the middle of the room, a white-draped figure. Oh, God, no. He turned and tried to get out but they were too fast for him. With a firm hand on either arm, they walked him to the table and the white-coated man standing there.

"This is Dr. Charlton," Tracey said. "Jack Wilson."

Dr. Charlton nodded briefly, then pulled back the sheet to expose the grey car rug still wrapped around Polly's head and shoulders.

"Do you recognize this blanket?" It was stained dark with blood, and dirt clung to the rough fabric everywhere.

"I don't . . . there are lots . . . it looks like the one I wrapped her in."

"Thank you." He folded back the blanket and pulled the sheet away from the rest of the body.

Wilson gagged and turned away.

"Take a good look, Jack," Inspector Goldsmith said. And they made him look again.

"Do you recognize this clothing as that of your wife, Mary Wilson?"

"Yes. It's an old country tweed she had." He was sorry he'd said so much.

"Do you recognize this body as that of your wife, Mary Wilson?" asked the coroner.

"Yes." His voice was faint.

"What did you say?" asked Dr. Charlton.

"Yes. That's her." And it seemed to Jack that the coroner took longer than he needed before he pulled up the sheet. The whole experience was horrible, and he said later that the police had no business to take him there with no warning and confront him with such an awful sight.

Goldsmith took Wilson out, and Tracey stayed for the post-mortem. Dr. Charlton gave notes to an assistant as he proceeded:

Length of body 5'3". Head turned to the right side. Body is clothed in what appears to be a woman's costume. Head and upper part of trunk is rolled up by a lap-rug. Body as a whole in bad state of decomposition. [The report goes into this in detail.] Feet enclosed in laced shoes medium height. Welt of shoe is brown kid, top of shoe grey suede, heels "French heels." Blue serge coat with belt, blue silk lining. Remains of a corsage pinned to left shoulder of the suit coat. Under the coat a white silk blouse buttoned down the front and fastened with a brooch at neck, appears to be a gold brooch, pearls and rubies, with one ruby hanging from centre as a pendant. Blue serge skirt to match the coat, skirt is buttoned with dome fasteners down front and left of centre. The blouse is flowered. Silk collar trimmed with lace at front of neck. Silk camisole buttoned down front. Name of maker on blouse "D'Allaird." Next a cotton embrasure. Then we come to the corsets with a safety pin on left breast at top, under corsets a cotton envelope [undergarment] stained with blood, then the body is disclosed.

The skull is badly shattered. Found against a fragment of skull a pellet of shot, flattened against it. The features are indistinct. The upper portion of the skull is missing, some of it, from roughly a line across the face under the eyes over the top of skull to a line drawn round the head at the lower lobe of the ears, the skull in between these lines is shattered into numerous pieces, the largest being 5 inches by nearly 3 inches, and it was in the inside of the largest fragment that the pellet was found. The shot was fired at close enough range that most of the charge went through, gas of charge has exploded inside. The forehead and dome of the skull is missing. No fragments of thin orbital plate. Under portion of the orbit is gone . . . On the skin of right side of nose there are three black marks suggestive of powder marks . . .

In the right hand side pocket of suit coat some papers were found which look like a sewing pattern. Piece of cotton wool found in left hand side of overcoat. No pocket or name tag in skirt. Woman is pregnant of male child 12 and a half inches long, about six months old. Woman has a good healthy heart, body drained of blood. Lungs healthy, liver healthy, stomach empty except for fragments of red apple skins. Stomach healthy. Intestines normal. Kidneys normal . . . A further examination of head showed a piece of bone down the neck at back. Shotgun pellet found in collar of coat on right side. Two more pellets were found in the scalp. A piece of straw was found in the hair. The hair was done up by 6 tortoise shell pins. Two "smitches" of hair found among natural hair. Deceased wore white silk stockings fastened by hose supporters to corsets.

The coroner's inquest was opened by Dr. Des Rosiers in McKague's Undertaking Rooms at 9:15 P.M. that night. Dr. Charlton was the only witness called. He gave evidence of his findings and stated that, in his opinion, the deceased came to her death from gunshot wounds in the head. The inquest was adjourned until 4:00 P.M. December 22.

Back once again at the Grand Hotel, Bill Tracey, accompanied by Corporal Chard, searched Wilson's trunks, looking for a jeweller's receipt for the purchase of Jessie's engagement ring. Polly Wilson's engagement ring was missing, and if there was no receipt, perhaps he had given the ring to Jessie. By now the police had decided they would put nothing past Jack Wilson. A careful search produced no receipt, but it produced something much more bizarre.

In the bottom of the second trunk lay a folded waterproof overcoat, apparently Wilson's, with both sleeves tied shut at the shoulder with a stout string in a sailor's knot.

"What the Sam Hill is this?" Tracey said.

"It looks like the coat has been submerged in water, doesn't it, sir?"

"It has been. Look at that string and the watermarks on it." He peered at it closely. "Hard to tell if these stains are all from water or something else he was trying to soak out."

They exchanged a look.

"But why tie up the sleeves?" asked Corporal Chard.

"Wilson could tell us, but he won't. My guess is he used it for something at the time of the murder." Tracey held it out. "Tied like this, it becomes a makeshift receptacle, doesn't it?"

"Good Lord. Why wouldn't he just get rid of it?"

"He's a Scot," said Tracey and laughed.

The police were intrigued by the coat. The lab verified it was blood Wilson tried to soak out. But why did he tie the sleeves shut?

According to the autopsy, many pieces of Polly Wilson's skull were missing and not found in the grave or at the site. Perhaps the coat was used as a receptacle for anything Wilson missed burying in the dark. Or he may even have used it to drag Polly's body to the grave site. Or both. They concluded he had tied the armholes shut while soaking it in an effort to keep it submerged in water. Both the blood-soaked dispatch case and topcoat could have been secreted in the straw suitcase Wilson took away with him. They would become exhibits at Wilson's trial.

Bill Tracey's crime report to Charles Mahony regarding the coat was also sent to Inspector Prime, RNWMP; the deputy attorney general; the agent of the attorney general; Inspector Smith, SPP; and Inspector Tait in Prince Albert. Things were getting complicated.

On December 16, Commissioner Perry advised the RNWMP comptroller that a charge of murder would be laid against Wilson.

Chapter XLI

⁀ BURIED BY STRANGERS ⁀

Things moved quickly. In Vancouver, two agents talked to Mrs. Sissons in her shop on Cordova Street about a man who sold her a hammerless, Scottish make shotgun on October 4. The description fit Wilson to a T, and the signature of J. Williams they believed to be Wilson's handwriting. They visited Mr. Mutch, who was reluctant to part with his gun, murder trial or no murder trial, police or no police, but eventually was persuaded. Commissioner Perry arranged for the weapon to be transported from Vancouver to Regina by an SPP noncommissioned officer.

James Hutchison cabled Superintendent Mahony, requesting that a lair be purchased and his sister be given a Christian burial, and all expenses sent to him. Sympathetic members of the St. Andrew's Society (a Scottish organization, most of them Presbyterian church members) purchased a casket. They held a small funeral service and stood respectfully as the minister committed Polly Wilson's body to its final rest. They also wrote letters of sympathy and Christian comfort to Polly's family.

Brutally murdered by the man she loved, Polly Wilson was finally buried by strangers in a strange land.

Jim Hutchison, incensed that Wilson should add insult to grievous injury by trying to blacken Polly's reputation, sent six letters attesting to his sister's upstanding, generous character. Jim's succinct letters, with their nice touch of irony when referring to Wilson, must have been a welcome change from Elizabeth's tragic, impassioned epistles. He had this to say about the maudlin letter from "dying sister Mary" extolling Wilson's sterling virtues:

> Keeping in view the fact that he invested all the money his parents left him in glass houses, that he was good to the poor people, erected a monument and chartered a pleasure steamer, it would be difficult to understand where the several thousand dollars for his wedding expenses came from . . . I note with considerable satisfaction from the Minister's letter that Mary did not have time to tell the half of what the poor boy suffered.

Elizabeth sent a letter telling about how good Polly had been to John's old uncle, the Joiner, and how his relations said she "might think much of herself as they never thought he would have given his stuffed fox away, he had prized it so much."

The Reverend Alan Reid of Slamannan parish church, who had married John and Polly, wrote that he had known Polly from childhood to womanhood:

> She was successively S.S. scholar, Junior Bible Class Treasurer and Collector for Church Objects in my congregation. I have never known nor heard of anything in her character or conduct that invited the least breath of criticism or suspicion. Her life in our midst was a blameless one. Her disposition was sweet and amiable. She was liked and trusted

by everyone who knew her; cheerfulness, good temper and good humour were so much a part of her nature that it would be difficult to imagine that she could bring anything but peaceableness and concord into the relations of the home she formed.

We, myself and those for whom I can speak, are deeply grieved to think that not only should she have met with so untimely an end, but that the attempt should have been made to cast a shadow on her memory.

The inquest resumed on December 22, 1919, in the Saskatoon courthouse, with Philip E. MacKenzie, K.C., representing the Crown.

Wilson was present, a livid scar on his throat standing out against his pale skin.

MacKenzie laid before him the statement he wrote in the guardroom.

"Did you make this statement, Mr. Wilson?"

Wilson stared into space.

"Is that your signature here on the last page?"

The defendant refused to answer.

Bill Tracey testified that, on December 11, Wilson phoned to say he wished to make a voluntary statement to reveal the whereabouts of Mary Wilson's body.

"Is this the statement you gave to Assistant Superintendent Tracey and Inspector Smith?" MacKenzie asked, laying the document before Wilson.

Wilson did not reply.

Inspector Smith testified to the discovery of the body in the place it was alleged to be, and that Wilson had identified the clothing as that worn by his wife at the time of her death.

No further evidence was taken.

The jury was out a short time and returned with the verdict: "That Mary Wilson came to her death in the P.M. of September 27, 1918. That Mary Wilson came to her death between Saskatoon and Rosthern. That Mary Wilson came to her death from a shot in the head fired at close range from a double-barrelled shotgun in the hands of John Wilson."

Chapter XLII

✐ A STRUGGLING MASS OF HUMANITY ✐

No one was prepared for it. Not the police, the legal counsel, court officials, or John Wilson. This was, after all, not a murder trial, but a preliminary hearing to determine if there was enough evidence for a trial. But there they were outside the courthouse, hundreds of curious citizens, their breath pluming the freezing air in a queue that wound on and on. They had begun lining up hours before.

When the doors opened at nine o'clock, the crowd surged forward, breaking rope cordons and jamming corridors, stairways and every available inch of standing room. Many were unable to get in at all. The Saskatoon *Daily Star* called it "a struggling mass of humanity intent on seeing John Wilson, alleged wife murderer." Saskatoon was not to see another scene to compare with it until the 1985 trial of Colin Thatcher for the same crime, murdering his wife.

Judge C. M. Johnson and Crown Prosecutor P. E. MacKenzie arrived and struggled through the crowd like salmon swimming upstream.

"Please, please," pleaded a flustered court official. "Make room for the magistrates to get through."

The courtroom was far too small to accommodate the several hundred spectators, and after a hurried consultation, it was announced that the hearing would adjourn to the Masonic Temple across the street.

The spectators then rushed to the temple, a large, two-storey building, where even the large assembly room in the basement proved much too small to hold them all. There were many women in the crowd, and some, like the men, stood on chairs in the back of the hall, craning their necks to catch a glimpse of Wilson.

An excited murmur went through the crowd as Wilson was led into the impromptu courtroom. His face was deathly pale and his hair long and dishevelled, but he walked unassisted and answered the few questions they would put to him with cheerful alacrity. He seemed fit, and his attitude represented a 180-degree turn from his behaviour at the inquest. When the court adjourned for luncheon, he trotted back to his cell through a back lane, with a guard hurrying beside him.

After lunch the crowd was even larger. The *Daily Star* reported that those who were there in the morning came back after lunch and brought their wives and families. When court resumed, the jammed courtroom heard from Isaac and John Neufeldt about the events on the morning of September 28, 1918.

Two photos of the burned car, which proved of great value to the police, were exhibited and identified by Isaac Peters.

"Why did you take the photos?" MacKenzie asked.

"It was the first car accident we had seen and we wanted a picture," Isaac replied.

Spectators laughed.

Mrs. Wismer's statement that Polly was six months pregnant when she left Regina brought a murmur from the spectators. She also told about Polly's finding Jessie's letter and leaving for Saskatoon to meet her husband. Mrs. Wismer explained that she had heard nothing from her since.

Assistant Superintendent Tracey testified to Wilson's two statements and attempted suicide.

Sergeant Drysdale and Sergeant Sparkman described finding the body. Pictures of the body at the burial site were shown, almost unrecognizable as human remains because of the large amount of frozen earth excavated. Then Dr. Charlton, the coroner, testified.

"And how, in your opinion, did the deceased, Mary Wilson, come to her death?" asked Prosecutor MacKenzie.

"She was killed by a shotgun blast which entered above the right eye and blew off the top of the head." Dr. Charlton replied.

The crowd gasped and a low buzz of talk erupted. Order was called, and MacKenzie then rested the enquiry.

"The prisoner will please stand," said the judge.

Wilson almost leapt to his feet.

"John Wilson, the charge against you is that on September 27, 1918, you did deliberately, and with malice aforethought, murder your wife, Mary Wilson, by a shotgun blast to the head. How do you plead?"

"Not guilty."

"Do you have legal counsel, Mr. Wilson?"

"No, I do not. And I don't want any."

"Do you wish to make any statement?"

"No, Your Worship," Wilson replied.

Magistrate Johnson then committed Wilson to stand trial at the next court of competent jurisdiction, the federal Court of King's Bench. He was to be remanded to the Prince Albert jail until the trial.

No one offered bail, and Wilson did not request it.

⌒

The next day, Wilson found himself on a familiar ride, the train bound for Prince Albert. He was accompanied this time by Inspector Smith.

How many times had he ridden this train on business and to be with Jessie that spring of 1918, with their love so new, intense, wondrous? How many times had she sat across from him or close beside him, he so proud to have her there? Now all was changed. Now winter lay over everything.

But at least he was going to Prince Albert, that much closer to her. They had promised to transfer him to the Prince Albert jail immediately if he told them where Polly was buried. They had promised at the same time to keep it out of the papers for Jessie's sake, and to arrange a meeting with her. All lies.

But still, now that he would be so close and away from the commotion in Saskatoon, surely she would come to see him. Surely she didn't hate him, he couldn't bear that.

Through the train windows the world went on as before: men laughing and loading freight at every station, station agents and train-men going about their business, passengers being met at each little town, bundled children on sleighs.

When the train stopped at Blaine Lake, his heart surged as he caught sight of John Patterson's livery barn, Jessie's house, the streets they had walked so many times together. He crossed the aisle and sat on the other side, his eyes closed. Eventually the train started up again.

Someone had left yesterday's *Daily Star* on the seat, and he read the account of his preliminary hearing. What a shock that had been, all those people. The paper's front page carried a story about the Treaty of Versailles: "The omission of America's signature stands for the bitter disappointment of the hope that glowed with promise a year ago," he read. The article might have been talking about him.

∽

On January 29, 1920, Elizabeth wrote to Commissioner Perry on black-bordered stationery to thank him for his kindness to the family. She couldn't read his or Superintendent Mahony's letters herself, she said; her husband had to read them to her and she was sure he left out the worst.

> Mrs. A. Wilson Fullwood (a cousin of Jack Wilson's) wants me to draw your attention to a matter in Wilson's last confession, namely, that he says my sister's ring had *one* stone, now it was a 5 stoned diamond ring, his engagement ring to her, her marriage ring was not very broad, but thick through and heavy. She had also a beautiful pendant and necklet and a brooch in the form of a spray of flowers composed of pearls and a small ruby or two. The latter was a present from her husband when they spent a holiday in Dublin and Killarney the Autumn after they were married. Then she had a lovely dark blue handbag, a gift she got when leaving for Canada and her suitcase was a large light brown patent leather one with leather and brass finishings—a gift from my husband and I. Mrs. Fullwood says I must write you about these things before it is too late to see about them as she says my sister's little girlie will value these more than all the world when she grows up.

Elizabeth ended the letter with gratitude to Commissioner Perry from herself and her family. Her father, she said, would yet forgive Wilson if he would tell the truth.

∽

In the Prince Albert jail, the prisoner waited. What went through his mind as he sat and smoked day after day in that jail cell? Did he get through each day on the hope of hearing from Jessie? Did he wait anxiously for the mail, listen for her footsteps, his heart quickening at each approach of the guard?

Wilson changed his mind about legal counsel and retained James

Hawkins Lindsay of Prince Albert. He may have chosen Lindsay for his name, coincidentally Jack's second name and the one he signed to some of his love letters to Jessie.

One thing was abundantly clear to Wilson: he could not lie his way out of this situation. His act was indefensible, and the only remote possibility of mercy might come through a plea of insanity. Jack Wilson therefore proceeded to act insane.

In a January affidavit, a frustrated James Lindsay stated that his repeated efforts to talk to Wilson met with failure as a result of Wilson's "ill health," or "his inability to give any intelligent answers to assist in his defence." Wilson was treading God's boards again, but this time they were crumbling beneath him. His absurd behaviour—muttering, mumbling, gesturing wildly, refusing to answer questions—succeeded only in making him look ridiculous. However, on January 23, Lindsay filed a notice of motion to the effect that his client had been unable to give proper instructions for his defence, that he had not sufficient time to prepare the same, that publication of a statement allegedly made by the accused would be prejudicial to him, and that there was an absence of material witnesses.

Prosecutors replied with sworn statements from Dr. Oswald Rothwell, who treated Wilson several times while at the Regina jail, attesting to Wilson's rational behaviour, and an affidavit from Charles McGregor, Prince Albert jailer, who had spoken with Wilson every day of his incarceration and who attested to Wilson's completely sane behaviour at all times. Upon both going to and coming from interviews with his lawyer, he acted completely normal, though his lawyer complained to McGregor that during those interviews Wilson gave no sensible answers. Dr. R. L. King, the jail doctor who had Wilson under observation from the time of his incarceration, also gave a statement as to his rational behaviour at all times.

∼

Jessie was now six months pregnant, at the same stage as Polly Wilson when her life ended. Jessie's pregnancy must have seemed interminable, with the father of her child jailed for murder and the whole appalling situation uppermost in her mind day and night.

James Hawkins Lindsay wrote to Jessie asking for any help she could give him—addresses of credible character witnesses, etc.—in forming her husband's defence. Jack had told him that Jessie could give him Conrad Read's address. Jessie answered the letter the same day, agreeing to get the address and to do whatever she could to help. But Con and Nell had moved, and she wasn't up to making inquiries through the police; it was all too humiliating. They could surely find out for themselves.

Just getting through her days must have been difficult enough without lawyers and police poking and prodding. And what could she tell them that they didn't already know? That she had been cruelly deceived by the man she loved, who she now knew was a murderer?

It was almost unbearable. The knowledge that Jack had murdered his wife and orphaned his children in order to be with her; that this woman, pregnant with yet another child, had been living with him in Regina as they planned their marriage; that many times she had driven over the very spot where Polly Wilson lay buried; that, in fact, Jack had made a special point of taking her along when he first went to the culvert with the men from the garage.

She was grateful for the support of her family, but knew that people in town talked of nothing else. What were they saying now? That she knew he still had a wife when she married him? That she knew what had happened by that culvert? Maybe even that.

And somehow she had to accept the fact that she had loved—perhaps still loved—the man who had done this loathsome thing. She may have believed Jack's protest that it was an accident. Perhaps she even still believed that Polly Wilson was a bad woman, at least partly at fault for pursuing Jack when he no longer wanted her. She had believed everything else.

∽

James Lindsay's efforts to have Wilson's trial delayed until the May sitting were unsuccessful. The doctor called to examine Wilson reported that he was fit to stand trial. And Lindsay's contention that newspaper reports of Wilson's alleged confession would damage his prospect of a fair trial fell on deaf ears. The trial was set for February 2, and on February 2 it would begin.

Chapter XLIII

∽ THE TRIAL ∾

Even more people than before waited outside the courthouse, but the scenes of disorder that marked the preliminary hearing did not reoccur. Potential jurymen, police officers and witnesses were admitted first. Then, after twelve men were chosen and the charge read, the remaining seats were given to the public. When the courtroom doors opened to admit the spectators, the sheriff's officers were prepared. They showed preference to the women in the line. When the courtroom filled to overflowing, more than two hundred people remained outside.

The judge and jury took their places, and the trial of the *Rex vs. John Wilson* opened in the Court of King's Bench, Chief Justice Sir Frederick Haultain presiding. The presence of a number of Mounted Police officers, their red tunics in vivid contrast to the khaki of the SPP, provided the courtroom with a dramatic and colourful touch. An item in the *Daily Star* that day reported that the RNWMP and the Dominion Mounted Police had merged under the common title of Royal Canadian Mounted Police.

A ripple went through the crowd as John Wilson was led into the prisoner's box by a jail guard. Wilson was pale and wild-eyed, his cheeks sunken. He had grown a light moustache, and his hair needed cutting.

Philip E. MacKenzie, K.C., was the Crown prosecutor. James Hawkins Lindsay, for reasons unknown, did not conduct Wilson's defence. That unenviable job fell to A. Murray McIntyre, assisted by Cecil Blackburn.

McIntyre opened the proceedings by challenging the jury: "In view of the great publicity that has been given this case, a great deal of which has been unfair to the accused, I would ask Your Lordship to have the jury challenged for cause."

Five of the jurymen were challenged. All five admitted having read newspaper reports of the case but all swore they had not been influenced by these reports, and were ready to give a verdict solely according to the evidence. Seven others were not challenged.

During the morning session, Wilson sat with his eyes fixed on the ceiling just above Chief Justice Haultain's chair. He scarcely moved, and then only to glance hurriedly at each new witness.

Philip MacKenzie opened his preliminary address to the jury. He stressed the serious nature of the case, involving, as it might, the life of a fellow creature. He explained murder, in the light of the law, differentiating it with other types of crime in which death was a result.

Then he carefully detailed the facts of the case from the time the defendant was a young man in Scotland. He recounted Wilson's marriage to Polly Hutchison, his immigration to Canada, enlistment in the RNWMP and his falling in love with Jessie Patterson. He told the hushed courtroom that it was Polly Wilson's fear for her husband's health that compelled her to make the long journey to Canada to care for him. He detailed their lives up to the time John Wilson met his wife at the Saskatoon station with a marriage licence in his pocket, and married Jessie Patterson two days later.

And the parade of witnesses began. Their testimony would take up the first two days of the trial.

Crown Prosecutor MacKenzie first called Eileen Wismer to the stand. He asked her to tell the court about the Wilsons' stay at her house, which she did, including Polly's discovery of Jessie's letter and her departure for Saskatoon with three hundred dollars pinned to her underclothing. She concluded her testimony by telling of Wilson's late night visit the week after Polly left, his story about the accident near Sutherland, and his asking if Polly had left behind a black purse and necklace.

The telegrams signed "Polly" and Wilson's letter to Mrs. Wismer about Polly being down with flu were produced, read by Philip MacKenzie, and entered as exhibits. Mrs. Wismer said she would scarcely recognize the man in the prisoner's box as the John Wilson who had stayed at her house.

Next witness was Mrs. Harry Hansen, who had occupied the room across from the Wilsons', and had accompanied Polly to the train when she left for Saskatoon. They had become friendly, and on one occasion, Polly had shown her two letters from Jessie Patterson to Jack. The defence strenuously objected to her revealing their contents, since the prosecution could not produce the letters. Chief Justice Haultain sustained the objection. Mrs. Hansen said she gave Polly a black handbag and a gold brooch as going away gifts. She told the court that although Polly didn't seem very happy to be joining her husband in Saskatoon, she bought a corsage before boarding the train and was excited about having her children with her soon.

Wilfred Sales, the Wheatley's Jewellery Store clerk, identified marriage licence #46645 as the one he sold to an anxious Dominion police officer the morning of Friday, September 27, 1918. Yes, he recognized the accused as that person.

Isaac Neufeldt testified to Wilson's early morning visit to his farm on September 28. He described the burning car, and his feeling that there was something funny about the whole thing. As did Isaac Peters and the other threshers, one after another. And Agnes Neufeldt, now a full seventeen years old, described the spray of blood on the straw suitcase in the back seat, and recalled that she asked Wilson what it was. "He sort of yanked the valise into the front and told us it was blood from the geese. He seemed mad that we asked."

John Neufeldt testified that he loaned Wilson a coat for the drive to Blaine Lake, and that Wilson had given him a new shovel he had "no more use for."

Alex Armstrong clearly remembered Jack's arrival at the hotel in the forenoon of September 28, looking like death warmed over. Wilson had gone into the main floor washroom, taking his rifle in with him, causing Alex to wonder what he was going to do in there. Under questioning from the Crown prosecutor, Armstrong recalled that Jack had told him in the summer of 1918 that his wife had died in the old country, and there was quite a story to her death, but that he never heard the story.

One after another they rose and walked to the witness box, each filling in a different part of the picture that had begun with such vague, shadowy images. As each new witness testified, the picture became clearer and sharper.

Reverend Wylie Clark described the late wedding ceremony in the Presbyterian manse. Mr. Riddell of Riddell's Carriage Works detailed Wilson's purchase of a new car, including the trip to the banker and Wilson's subsequent stories when the payments were missed. Jean Brown, Riddell's stenographer, spoke of Wilson's extreme nervousness when he returned with Jessie; Mrs. Amelia Foster, the newlyweds' landlady in Saskatoon, answered questions regarding the Wilsons' arrival, their stay at her house, and their departure for the west. Some of the other witnesses called were James Martin, Charlie McLean and Superintendent West, who found Polly's trunks. Sergeant Cather spoke about the events in Vancouver that opened the investigation into Mary Wilson's disappearance.

Detective Sergeant Drysdale, RNWMP, and Inspector Smith, SPP, recounted the exhumation of Polly Wilson's body. Sergeant Drysdale identified the photographs he took at the burial site. These were then added to the other exhibits.

Then Dr. Charlton gave the results of his autopsy on Mary Wilson's body. Several articles of women's clothing and a ladies' boot were examined and identified by Dr. Charlton as those he had removed from the victim's body. After graphically describing the head wound, he produced a vial containing lead pellets that he had taken from the head, and the spectators leaned forward to see better. Mrs. Wilson had been six months' pregnant with a male child. He had found no money on Mary Wilson's body but there had been a large safety pin pinned to her underclothing for no obvious purpose.

Assistant Superintendent Tracey testified to finding the dispatch case in Wilson's trunk and the almost one hundred letters to Jessie Patterson. The blood-stained dispatch case was displayed, and Dr. Charlton testified that the substance staining the case and some of the personal letters inside it was human blood. Some of the blood-stained love letters were read by the prosecutor. The courtroom was silent. This was the drama they had all come to hear.

On the second day Wilson seemed much worse. He huddled, open-mouthed and wild-eyed, in the prisoner's box as the one witness after another was sworn in and related another part of the story. He mumbled to himself constantly. When court adjourned for lunch the second day, Wilson stumbled and groped his way along the rail of the jury box.

Several times Chief Justice Haultain objected to the length of the Crown's evidence. "There is too much atmosphere," he protested, "I am sure this is not all essential."

The Crown prosecutor promised to endeavour to be more to the point.

Sergeant James Cather, Southey and Walt Kelland testified. Sergeant W. M. Jennings of the Provincial Police, stationed at Hafford, identified the black purse and brooch—Mrs. Hansen's farewell gifts to Polly—as items he had received at the Patterson home in Blaine Lake on December 29, 1919. This disclosure caused a buzz of whispers among the spectators, soon silenced by a look from the judge. When the case for the defence was heard next day, John Wilson would surely be questioned by the prosecutor about these items and about when he had given them to Jessie.

Jessie Wilson was listed as a witness for the defence, but she did not appear.

Forty-two witnesses in all told what they knew to that packed courtroom. By the time they were finished there was no doubt in anyone's mind about what took place at that culvert near Waldheim. The case for the Crown was complete, the picture there for all to see. Clear, sharp, and hung up to dry.

Those who could not be in the courtroom waited eagerly for the newspaper reports each day, which covered the trial in great detail. The case for the defence was to begin on the third morning of the trial.

Chapter XLIV

✿ A PROFESSIONAL MAN ✿

A man who followed the trial from afar with great interest was Arthur Ellis, whose real name was Arthur Bartholomew English. Ellis was a professional hangman, though that was a title he disliked, since he considered himself an artist of the highest order. He called himself the Official Executioner to the Dominion of Canada. As his "artistic discipline" was not overcrowded, Ellis presided at most hangings, certainly those of high-profile criminals.

Ellis was a mild-looking, dapper Englishman, in round, thick-lensed spectacles, who always dressed in a neat suit, tie and soft fedora. He looked like a kindly district doctor or an avuncular travelling Watkins man with a sample case. But Ellis's black bag was not filled with vanilla or cough syrup or cinnamon for apple pies; it held an assortment of measuring tapes, scales, black hoods and ropes.

Ellis complained, quite rightly, of unfair treatment. "If a hotelman learns I'm in his house, he asks me to vacate it. I am but one cog in the machinery of justice, and I am entitled to just as much respect as the Justice of the Assize Court." Ellis was a sociable, gregarious man, and it hurt him that others would shun him because of his profession. His mission was to carry out the letter of the law with as little suffering as possible to the condemned man or woman.

A professional he certainly was. He could glance at a man and tell his weight within a fraction of a pound. He could also tell how much drop to give him in the rope, and how long it would take for his circulatory system to stop functioning after his neck was broken. When he executed an infamous murderer, Henry Wagner, "The Flying Dutchman," he shaved eleven seconds off the record time between when a condemned man's foot touches the courtyard gravel to when the trap was sprung—just forty-seven seconds. The previous record was held by his uncle, a hangman in England. It was also something of a fetish with him that he ask each condemned person if he or she wished to make a confession before he carried out the sentence.

Arthur Ellis read the newspaper accounts of the Wilson trial with great interest. His expected that his services would soon be required in Saskatchewan.

Chapter XLV

~ A STRANGER IN A STRANGE LAND ~

On the third day the queue was longer still. The case for the defence would begin, with Wilson himself slated to testify.

Defence counsel A. M. McIntyre opened his battle for Wilson's life by introducing the statement Wilson gave in which Mary Wilson's death was described as a hunting accident.

Among the chief witnesses for the defence was Conrad Read. He had worked with John Wilson in two police forces, and he had nothing but good things to say about his character and the way he discharged his duties as a police officer. Under cross-examination, he said that on September 26 Wilson had asked him to have the car ready by four o'clock next day, as Wilson was going to Blaine Lake to get married. He planned to be married that evening.

Other witnesses for the defence were men who had served in the Military Police in Regina, including Wilson's superintendent, who readily attested to his dedication to his work and his good character. Officers in the RNWMP also testified to Wilson's good character. William H. Stoddart, who served with Wilson in 1915, said he'd always heard that Wilson had a good reputation. G. S. Jobin gave testimony to the good character held by Wilson in the Military Police. (This is the same man who told Sergeant Drysdale that he thought Wilson a "rum customer.") Alex Armstrong from the Blaine Lake Hotel testified that he had never had a moment's trouble with Jack, who paid his bills promptly and was pleasant to have around.

McIntyre also cross-examined Assistant Superintendent Tracey regarding whether Wilson had told him an uncle in Scotland had attempted suicide and died in an insane asylum. Tracey said Wilson had not told him that. This was the first mention of insanity at the trial. The defence also called the police to task for their treatment of Wilson in their efforts to make him confess and to tell where he had buried his wife.

"In fact," said McIntyre, "you used third-degree tactics to elicit information from the accused. You put him through the sweatbox, didn't you?"

"We did not," replied the laconic Tracey. "I don't know what a sweatbox is. I never saw one."

The moment the spectators were waiting for arrived. McIntyre called John Wilson to the stand.

Wilson heard his name called. Trembling violently, he shook his head and refused to get to his feet. When the guard tried to help him out of his chair, Wilson shrank away from him. After a hurried consultation with the lawyers, Chief Justice Haultain announced that the prisoner would be taken out of the courtroom and examined by Dr. John A. Valens.

Shaking visibly and pointing mutely to the ceiling, Wilson was led from the courtroom. Presumably, by pointing to the sky, Wilson was invoking God as witness to his innocence. Back in the holding room, Dr. Valens administered a sedative to his terrified patient.

No one left the courtroom; there were only the sounds of whispering and coughing, and the scraping of chairs as people turned around to discuss this new development with the person behind.

In ten minutes, the guard arrived with a message from Dr. Valens. John Wilson was in no condition to give evidence at the moment, but the doctor believed he could have him in shape to do so in an hour's time.

McIntyre was excused to consult with his client. On his return to the courtroom, McIntyre asked Judge Haultain for time to bring his client around.

"He says his mind is all right but he is too sick to give evidence, Your Honor," McIntyre said.

"I am anxious to give you every opportunity to defend your client," said the Chief Justice. "I realize the difficulties you have to overcome." Haultain adjourned court until 2:00 P.M.

When court resumed, McIntyre said he regretted that his client was still unable to give the evidence counsel had desired him to give. He asked permission to recall Assistant Superintendent Tracey to the stand. He could give the evidence he had hoped would be forthcoming from the accused.

Tracey testified as to the contents of Wilson's second statement, in which he described a hunting accident as the cause of his wife's death, and how he had finally decided to bury her under the culvert, fearing no one would understand. It also detailed the terror that beset him after the death of his wife, and gruesomely described his attempt at suicide.

McIntyre then read Wilson's statement very carefully to the jury. He contended that hunting accidents were very common, so common, in fact, that the government had passed legislation making it an offence to carry a loaded weapon in a vehicle. He further contended that Wilson's actions were, given the circumstances and his state of panic, believable.

He then questioned Bill Tracey again about insanity in Wilson's family, but Tracey said he did not remember Wilson telling him about a mentally ill uncle. "But I asked him regarding insanity in his family, and he said there was some."

Philip MacKenzie then rose to ask the witness a question.

"All the time you saw him, he was rational, wasn't he?" he asked.

"He was a most sensible man. More so than lots of others," replied Tracey.

When the defence counsel said he had no more witnesses, Judge Haultain asked Prosecutor MacKenzie to address the jury first. McIntyre then attempted to block proceedings by stating there was nothing in evidence to prove that the shooting took place in this jurisdiction. The judge said it was too late for that now.

Crown Attorney Philip MacKenzie opened his address to the jury: "There are two central points in this case—around the twenty-seventh of September 1918, and following November eleventh, 1919. The first is the time of the alleged crime and the second is the period when investigations were made leading to the accused's arrest."

He dwelt on Wilson's relations with Jessie Patterson and the unexpected arrival of Polly Wilson.

"She came, a stranger in a strange land, leaving her two children in

Scotland. Wilson's affections had grown cold and she tried to win back his love—a love that had been transferred to Jessie. Wilson tried to keep her presence in this country quiet and all the time paid attention to the girl in Blaine Lake. This woman in Regina was a burden on him. He turned down a chief inspectorship at Regina to come to Saskatoon near Jessie.

"Another thing, Polly was to give birth to a child, making it increasingly difficult for him to continue with Jessie . . . Instead of telling Polly he could not live with her, he took advantage of the fact that she was his wife and put her in the family way. Seeing that he was about to be burdened with an offspring as well, he formed a definite plan.

"In a murder case it is necessary to prove intention . . . in this case you have ample opportunity to ascertain intention, there are so many letters bearing on this angle. He wrote to Polly to take the train at a definite time. Why, at the same time, did he write Jessie telling her he was going out for a marriage licence and to secure 'our rooms' in Nutana?

"What was the man's intention? Was he going to marry Jessie? He states in his confession he had to marry her legally. There were only two ways he could do it legally. Through a divorce or through the death of his first wife.

"It was while Mary was hastening to Saskatoon to meet John Wilson that he was busy at Wheatley's Jewellery Store getting a licence to marry Jessie Patterson, swearing himself to be a bachelor.

"He met Mary. There is no contradiction to that. Why did he take her into the country? He had a marriage licence in his pocket and was on his way to Blaine Lake. Surely he did not want her present at his marriage with Jessie . . .

"If the shooting was an accident, Wilson's subsequent actions do not suggest it. He had no grief for the woman who has borne him two children. He seeks no medical aid. Instead, he buries her four feet underground and a few hours after marries Jessie. If the man has lost his wife by accident, out of decency he would have put off his second nuptials a little while longer. Later, those who knew Mary are led by Wilson to presume she was still alive.

"Why did he take a post office box at Sutherland? Wasn't it to guard against Jessie finding out he was not a divorced man? At the very time Wilson told Regina friends that Mary was at Sutherland with influenza, she was in her grave and he was living with Jessie. Telegrams didn't come from Polly. She was dead. They were signed by Wilson."

The prosecution read numerous letters and telegrams all written after Mary's death, but written as if she were alive, at one time sick with flu, convalescent and then having given birth to a child.

"Gentlemen, Polly Wilson wasn't ill with influenza. She did not give birth to a child. She was not going home. She was dead, dead by the hand of the man who wrote intimate epistles telling of her progress and recovery.

"When he rejoined the RNWM Police in 1919, he gave his wife's name as Mary because that was what he had told them in 1914."

Philip MacKenzie rested the case for the Crown.

McIntyre next rose to address the jury. His address was understand-ably briefer. But the Saskatoon *Daily Star* reported that evening that McIntyre "with only slight material with which to work—Wilson's statement that the shooting was an accident—he had put together an admirable defence for Wilson, and a plea for acquittal that called forth the admiration of the court. The chief justice sincerely thanked Mr. McIntyre for the way in which he·conducted the case for the accused man."

Then Sir Frederick Haultain addressed the jury: "Wilson's dealings with Jessie Patterson mark him a scoundrel but you are not trying him for being a scoundrel. The question is for you to decide whether his wife died as the result of an accident or was she murdered and if Wilson committed the crime . . . You are not to find Wilson guilty of one thing because he acted like a scoundrel in another. Your indigna-tion is pardonable, but you must not allow it to influence your verdict. The accused is entitled to the benefit of the doubt."

The jury retired at 4:30 P.M. on the third day of the trial.

In the penultimate crime report on the case, made on February 5, Detective Sergeant Sparkman addressed Wilson's claim that he was too sick to give evidence himself.

In contradiction of the latter contention, I beg to state that when the accused was taken to his cell, to await the decision of the Jury, he lost the vacant stare he wore in the courtroom. He sat on the bed and in a quite composed manner took a packet of cigarettes from his right hand coat pocket and borrowed a match from the guard to light it. He went on smoking. He then looked up at the guard and said some words to the effect "that he guessed the dope worked on him," probably referring to the injection given him by Doctor J. Valens.

The jury was out less than two hours. At word of the jury's return, the spectators rushed back into the courtroom. Many had never left. John Wilson was led back into the dock, once again adopting the manner he'd presented in the courtroom.

At the request of Chief Justice Haultain, the jury foreman stood.

"And how do you find the prisoner, John Wilson? Guilty or not guilty?"

"Guilty, Your Honour."

Sir Frederick turned to Wilson.

"John Wilson, you have been found guilty of the crime with which you are charged. Have you anything to say why sentence should not be passed upon you?"

A startling change came over Wilson. He sprang to his feet. Gone was the listless attitude, the dull, roving stare, the expression of imbecility. In a clear voice that could be heard in all parts of the courtroom, he said, "Yes, sir. I wish to protest against the low-down dirty methods of the police in taking advantage of my condition of mind and body to obtain information from me."

"Is that all?" asked the judge.

"Yes, sir."

"John Wilson," said Judge Haultain, "the sentence of this court will be that you will be taken from here to Prince Albert jail where you will be kept until the twenty-third day of April, when you will be taken and hanged by the neck until you are dead, and may God have mercy on your soul."

Wilson was apparently little moved by the death sentence. Sergeant

Sparkman accompanied Wilson and the guard to his cell in the court-house basement, where Wilson at once lay full length on the bed.

"Well, John, how do you feel?" the guard asked after a few moments.

"I don't care now," Jack replied.

The prisoner ate with apparent appetite his supper of coffee, bread and butter and canned cherries. Afterwards he lit a cigarette and smoked with composure.

He slept soundly without stirring for nearly nine hours that night. He was awakened at 5:45 for his breakfast, which he also ate with appetite, and walked briskly to the early morning north-bound train for his last ride to Prince Albert.

On the way down to the station, he volunteered the statement, "Well, my mind's much easier now I have got my sentence."

"It's a relief to you, is it, John?" asked the guard.

"Yes. It feels like a great weight has been lifted off my shoulders."

His response seems to imply that he wanted to atone for his crime. This would be in keeping with his statement "I always thought I would see it through," and with not destroying the evidence that would convict him.

At Prince Albert, he was placed in the death cell, where he would receive more consideration than the other prisoners for the last few weeks of his life. Seventy-seven days.

⌢⌣

Superintendent Mahony sent Polly's family a transcript of the trial and a copy of Wilson's last statement, written in the Prince Albert jail. Elizabeth replied. Here are some excerpts from her letter written on March 29, 1920.

I feel as if I would never get over it, one thing I know my father and mother will never get over it. It's the awful thought that he who pro-fessed to love her so much could do such a crude and cruel deed and rob his own little ones of their darling mother. Yet with all, we pity him greatly to think he has brought himself to such a pass. Oh, Sir! it's awful to think of his dreadful end and to know that he could have been so happy had he done right. If only he had spared her life she had a pair of the most capable hands and could have worked for herself and her children . . .

His last statement, these are all false as is the amount of money he says my sister had when she landed. She would have had at least 100 pounds if not more. She got a great many presents in money as parting gifts from friends and relatives . . . We were not aware that Mrs. Hansen had given Polly jewelry as a gift, but Mrs. Laing told Mother that Polly had bought a beautiful pendant to send to my sister Nellie for Christmas . . . I note that J. Patterson gave you some of this jewelry, and note you ask us not to wrongly blame her. I can assure you we don't blame her. We have nothing but pity for her. He has deceived and lied to her and ruined her life, but at the same time, like Wilson's own relations, I think she ought to be thankful for she has had a merciful escape. He tired of everybody and everything and he would soon have tired of her. He was going to blow his brains out if Father refused to give him Polly, yet see what he has done . . . Oh, how she loved John Wilson, the worst I ever heard her say about him was "Oh, if Jack would only write."

We are going to take further advantage of your pro-offered kindness in asking you to send my dear sister's belongings here addressed to my home . . . but not to send any of the clothes, etc. she wore when she lost her life . . . Indeed, Sir, I dread the coming of her things for I helped her pack with oh such prayers and hopes for her future happiness.

Accept again our united thanks (as a family) for your extreme kindness and sympathy to us in our great bereavement . . .

Elizabeth Craig

Chapter XLVI

✐ I DID NOT KNOW WHAT I WAS DOING ✐

We don't know what John Wilson did for those seventy-seven days, what letters he wrote or received, who came to see him, what thoughts occupied his mind. He did not contact any of his or Polly's family or inquire about his children or about who would look after them in the years ahead. There is no record of Jessie's having visited him after the verdict, although she may well have done so.

On March 1, he gave yet another interminable statement—the one Elizabeth referred to in her letter—this before Sheriff David Seath, and jail warden Charles McGregor. Like the others, it was a rambling account of events since the trouble started in Scotland. It was full of lies about how much money he was sending Polly all along and excuses for not turning in the fines he collected under the Military Service Act. His "mind was all to pieces." His "head was all gone." He had "fits of insanity." And on and on.

About the day of the murder he makes this admission: "I pulled the trigger intentionally, but I did not know what I was doing. She was sitting in the front of the car looking right towards me . . . I don't know whether I pulled one trigger or two triggers."

Polly Wilson knew, in that split instant before the blast, that her husband was going to kill her.

Given the state of Wilson's mind at that time, one can almost grasp what he meant when he said he did it but he didn't know what he was doing.

Wilson recounted his attempts at suicide after he and Jessie were married. He claimed he was not drinking at the time he was in Saskatoon while several witnesses testified that he was drinking heavily. He told of blacking out east of Regina at Grand Coulee and stopping a car and getting a lift back to barracks just before reveille. He told it as proof of insanity, but it sounds very much like an alcoholic blackout.

He aired his grievance about the police:

> They questioned me something terrible . . . about where they would find the body, but I would not tell them, and told them I would not tell them until I could see Jessie and tell her myself . . . and I think it was Goldsmith who put up an awful story about the Body lying out all that time in the cold . . .
>
> Then I told him I would tell him the whole truth about everything, if he would keep it out of the newspapers and transfer me to the Prince Albert

Jail right away and give me a chance to see Jessie before it went to the newspapers so that I could tell her everything, so that she could write to my people in the Old Country and tell them everything . . . then they . . . took me to Saskatoon [and] down to some place, . . . and before I knew where I was they had me confronted with the Body, to identify the clothing . . . Next morning Tracey brought me to Prince Albert and meantime they published full details and Jessie was worse than ever she was.

Jack Wilson apparently saw nothing odd in asking Jessie to write to his people "and tell them everything." It seems he had no conception of what a terrible assignment that would be.

He also tried to explain what happened to Polly's money and jewellery:

One of the witnesses at the trial stated that my wife had $300 pinned inside her dress when she left Regina, but I never knew anything about that, and do not believe she had the money, she had about £10 when she arrived in this country . . . Some days after 27th September I found my wife's purse in my pocket, and I must have taken her two rings off, and put them there along with three or four dollars and some coppers. One ring got lost, the other ring and the purse and some jewellry in the purse I left undisturbed until the police got it. The other ring was lost. I do not know when or where. They tried to make out I gave it to Jessie, but I did not, as my wife's ring had five or six stones, and the one Jessie has has only the one stone.

Wilson's signature on his last statement is about half the size of his signature on the marriage licence.

∼

In Blaine Lake, with her pregnancy almost full term, Jessie waited for April 23. The wait was agonizing. She couldn't stop thinking about Jack and his terrible fate. And, of course, as the time drew near, it also drew nearer to the day she would give birth to their child. Each day those two momentous events came closer. Along with the natural fears of a first-time mother, and one with no husband at her side, she also had to carry the picture of Jack walking to the scaffold and up the steps to his horrible death.

A series of letters regarding the return of two trunks which had been held in evidence at the trial, give some clue to her feelings.

Six days before his sentence was to be carried out, Wilson signed this request.

Prince Albert Jail

April 17, 1920

I hereby request that the four trunks presently in Saskatoon, and which were used as Exhibits at my trial, be forwarded to my wife, Mrs. John Wilson, Blaine Lake.

John Wilson

Two of the trunks were Jack and Jessie's; the other two were the trunks Polly Wilson packed in Regina, the ones the police found in the express office. He wanted them all sent to Jessie.

Government of the Province of Saskatchewan

Office of the Sheriff—Judicial District of Prince Albert

April 23rd, 1920

H. Ludgate, Esq.,

Clerk of the Court,

Saskatoon, Sask.

Dear Sir:

Referring to your letter of 13th inst., respecting the disposal of four trunks containing personal effects which were the property of John Wilson.

On receipt of your letter I visited Wilson, but he would give me no instructions until his wife called. His wife did not call to see him, altho she promised me to do so on Monday or Wednesday of this week. As I anticipated something of this nature I took an order from Wilson authorizing the trunks to be forwarded to Mrs. John Wilson, Blaine Lake. I enclose you the order and presume you will act on his request.

>Your obedient servant,
>D. Seath
>Sheriff

This letter was written on the day of Wilson's execution.

The clerk of the court sent Jessie a letter on April 26 advising that the trunks would be forwarded at her instruction. She replied:

>Blaine Lake, Sask.
>April 28/20

Mr. H. Ludgate
Saskatoon, Sask.
Dear Sir,
Your letter at hand today concerning the trunks. I do not want that woman's trunk sent here, no matter what the order was, it will I think be easy to tell from the others as it will likely be labelled from Scotland to Regina and name and etc. You can send it back to where it came from or do anything you like with it.

I will be very glad to get the others as soon as possible.

Trusting to receive the above at an early date and thanking you.

>I remain,
>Yours truly,
>Mrs. Jessie Wilson

Jessie does not call Mary Wilson by name, but "that woman"; and her instruction to "send it back to where it came from or do anything you like with it" seems to imply a deep resentment. Jessie's future must have looked very bleak indeed.

Polly Wilson and the children were not the only victims.

>Blaine Lake, Sask.
>June 20/20

Clerk of the Judicial Dist.
Saskatoon.
Dear Sir,

I wish to state that when I received my two trunks from Saskatoon there were several articles missing besides some valuable papers and letters which I wish you would return.

I wrote the Prov. Police about these and they referred me to you. Besides the papers and letters which I must have as there are some receipts in those which I want, there was a gentleman's signet ring of heavy gold and the initial R. W. K., also a gold tie holder and six yards of blue silk.

Trusting you will give this your prompt attention,

I remain,

Yours truly,

Mrs. Jessie Wilson

Judging by the sheriff's letter dated April 23, John Wilson had waited in vain that last week for a visit from his darling Jessie.

Chapter XLVII

~ CASE CLOSED ~

The Prince Albert jail looked down upon Prince Albert from the top of a hill at the end of Central Avenue.

At 6:50 A.M. on April 23, 1920, the death bell began to toll, momentarily stilling the sparrows celebrating spring in the trees outside the jail.

Sheriff Seath and Arthur Ellis entered Wilson's cell, where Wilson was drinking a cup of coffee. He had refused breakfast.

"Do you wish to make a confession, Jack?" Arthur Ellis asked in a kindly voice.

"No," Jack replied.

"Your time has come, John," Sheriff Seath told him.

Wilson put down the cup, and Ellis pinioned his hands behind him. His hands kept opening and shutting, the only sign of his nervousness; that and his deathly pallor. Waiting outside in the corridor were Charles McGregor, the warden, and the Reverend J. MacDonald.

Although no reporters were allowed in the courtyard, those standing outside that morning must have felt a chill as the bell slowly knelled the procession to the gallows.

As the small knot of men in the jail corridor turned right towards the courtyard, Wilson's calm faltered. His mouth worked convulsively; he stumbled as his feet touched the gravel of the courtyard and the gallows came into view. Standing in the courtyard with hats removed were Dr. P. D. Tyerman and Inspector R. R. Tait. Wilson regained his calm and followed Ellis up the steps. Ellis's was the last face Jack Wilson would look upon.

The hood dropped.

At 6:55 A.M. the bell stopped and the black flag ran up the pole. Life was pronounced extinct at 7:07 A.M.

∾

The last crime report on the case of "Mary Wilson, Missing" was filed by the Saskatchewan Provincial Police that day.

"Case Completed," wrote Sergeant S. H. Kistruck.

∾

In the records of the Department of Vital Statistics for April 23, 1920, is registered the death of John L. Wilson.

Also registered on that day is the birth of a son to John Wilson and Mrs. Jessie Wilson.

Epilogue
∽ HILLS AND VALLEYS ∾

Commissioner Charles Mahony is preparing his fourth report of the Saskatchewan Provincial Police to the attorney general. For several nights now, he has been reviewing the troubled year of 1920. The guns across the water were stilled a year ago, the Spanish flu had run its course, though there were sporadic outbreaks over the year, but the longed-for stability and prosperity have not returned. There is much unemployment, much resentment among the empty-eyed men who escaped the quagmire of no man's land to stand in long lines for a few hours work. It will take a long time to recover from the last few years. And where there is unemployment, there is crime. Charles Mahony's job has not been an easy one in 1920, but he would not want it if it was. His typewriter clatters in the empty building.

Rex vs. John Arthur. Kindersley District
The above named was charged with the murder of Harry d'Orguerre of Glidden, Saskatchewan. Evidence given at the Court of King's Bench at Kindersley on May 11th, 1920 before His Lordship, Justice McKay, tended to show that the death was the result of a fight after drinking. The Jury returned a verdict of "Not Guilty."

Rex vs. John Kozi
The above named appeared at the Court of King's Bench, Saskatoon, on November 5th, 1920, before Chief Justice Sir Frederick Haultain. Evidence showed that accused was employed by one George Simon, a farmer of Viscount. Some trouble ensued, as it was claimed, the deceased refused to pay accused his wages. Accused then shot Simon dead with a shotgun and later surrendered to the Police.
The Jury returned a verdict of "Guilty" and accused was sentenced to be hanged, a recommendation to mercy was made by the Jury.

Mahony looks out the window. The city is shrouded in an icy fog, white smoke from every chimney suspended in the frigid night. The soft aureoles of street lights scarcely illumine the occasional dark figure hurrying along the sidewalk, and a fresh snowfall muffles the sound of an automobile passing below the window. Mahony sighs and turns back to the pile of legal-size papers growing on the large oak desk. He is almost finished. There is only one case left.

Rex vs. John Wilson. Saskatoon District
This case will go down in the annals of crime as being one of the most dastardly murders ever committed in Western Canada and the disappearance of Mary Polly Wilson might still have been a mystery had it not been for the self-determination of a Scots woman, namely Mrs. Elizabeth Craig, a sister of the deceased. It is utterly impossible to give anything more than a very vague outline of the case in this report.

Mr. Filson Young, author of many books on notable English trials, in his introduction to "Trial of H. H. Crippen" states: "Most of the interest and part of the terror of great crime are due not to what is abnormal, but to what is normal in it; what we have in common with the criminal, rather than that subtle insanity which differentiates him from us, is what makes us view with so lively an interest a fellow-being who has wandered into these tragic and fatal fields. A mean crime, like that of the brute who knocks an old woman on the head for the sake of the few shillings in her store, has a mean motive; a great crime, like that of the man who murders his wife and little children and commits suicide because he can see only starvation and misery before them, gathers desperately into itself in one wild protest against destiny what is left of nobility and greatness in the man's nature. It is not that his crime has any more legal justification than that of the murdering robber; it has not. On the contrary, it is more of an outrage upon life, and far more damaging in its results upon the community. Yet we do not hate or execrate the author; we profoundly pity him; it is even possible sometimes to recognize a certain terrible beauty in the motive that made him thus make a complete sweep of his little world when it could no longer cope with the great world.

"There are, at the least, reasons for a great crime; for a mean one there are, at the most, excuses. The region of human morality is not a flat plain; there are hills and valleys in it, deep levels and high levels; there are also certain wild isolated crags, terrible in their desolation, wrapped in storms and glooms, upon which, nevertheless, a slant of sunshine will sometimes fall and reveal the wild flowers and jewelled mosses that hide in their awful clefts.

"Somewhere between these extremes, far below the highest, but far above the lowest, lies the case of Dr. Crippen, who killed his wife in order to give his life to the woman he loved. His was that rare thing in English annals, a crime passionel."

The Wilson murder resembles the Crippen case in very many respects. The motive in both instances was similar. Wilson, however, dared to go further than Crippen in that he married the woman for whom he so foully committed murder.

Here, Mahony gives a lengthy summing up of the case and a short summary of the trial. Then he continues:

Mary Polly Wilson appears to have been a splendid type of woman and the fact of her leaving her two children in Scotland and making the journey to Canada alone for the purpose of being with her husband proves that she was a true and faithful wife.

During the time of the investigation and even up to the present, numerous letters were received from Mrs. Wilson's parents and relations in Scotland, and from others who knew her well. Two of these letters I append herewith which will give you an idea of the respect and esteem in which the deceased was held . . .

Elizabeth Craig would have been pleased.

∽ AFTERWORD ∾

Fifteen years ago while working in a second-hand bookstore, I read a historical booklet called *Murder in Uniform*, by Christina Stewart and Lynn Hudson. It told the story of John Wilson, the only member of the RNWMP, including the RCMP, to ever be tried and executed for a crime. It had all the elements for an intriguing film, but not knowing what to do about that, I put the idea away. But the story wouldn't go away. Every so often I'd tell it to someone, and no one had ever heard of this fascinating piece of Saskatchewan history. Then in 1992 I told the story to Rob Sanders, publisher at Douglas & McIntyre Ltd., who said, "That's a wonderful story. You write it and we'll publish it."

In order to do that, I needed much more information, and wasn't finding it. Then Glenn Wright, a historian at the RCMP headquarters in Ottawa, suggested I ask for File #3275, Volumes 1 through 4, at the National Archives in Ottawa. This I did while in Ottawa for meetings of the Writers' Union of Canada in 1993. At the archives they produced four full boxes of files all labelled "John Wilson Murder—Waldheim." Needless to say, I didn't get to any Writers' Union meetings that weekend, and I stayed over an extra two days reading and tagging pages for photocopying.

It was all there, beginning with the impassioned, pain-filled letters from Elizabeth Craig to the police, begging for news of her sister, to the last crime report filed on the day John Wilson was hanged. A multiplicity of crime reports and letters by the RNWMP and the SPP, urgent coded telegrams, Wilson's forged letters to Jessie, his letters to Polly's family, the autopsy report, Wilson's statements and much more were in those boxes. In the last file in the last box was a large manila envelope—the kind that closes with a string looped in a figure 8—full of passionate love letters from John Wilson to Jessie Patterson and a few from her to him. When I finished reading through all this material, I knew I had to write the book.

But why would I write my first non-fiction book about this particular story, of all the stories out there? asked another writer. Not until then did I realize how much this story resonated for me personally. It took place, or much of it did, in small-town Saskatchewan, where I grew up. My father, Ed Binns, who immigrated to Canada from Kentucky as a young man, was a great storyteller, and many of the stories he told were about the early days in Saskatchewan and the Mounted Police. He was fascinated by that colourful history. I thought of him often as I wrote the book, and wished I could tell him about it. I passed so many hours of my childhood at his desk in the Pool elevator office in Mervin, drawing on old grain ticket books with indelible pencils, and listening to the voices of rural prairie men. Those voices are as natural to me as breathing, and there are many in this book.

And as I wrote about Polly Wilson I thought often of my grandmother, Annie Thomson, who came to Ontario from Scotland as a young woman. I realized for the first time how many of her customs and habits came from her Scots background. She was a courageous, resourceful woman with a strong faith, and like Polly Wilson, she worked as a seamstress before she married my grandfather.

My mother told me she remembered my grandparents talking about the Wilson case. They kept clippings of it, and since I read everything in that house, it's likely I read about this story fifty years ago. To answer my friend's question, I chose this story to write (or it chose me) not only because it's such a good one, but also because I felt at home in it.

From the time I started working on the book, I'd wanted to see Scotland, but could not afford to go. In February 1995, my son, Scott Simmie, was home for a visit from Moscow, where he produced the news for CBC. He presented me with a ticket to Scotland and said, "You still have time to see these places you're writing about." I went on April 1, and I did see those places for myself; the village of Slamannan, in lovely, hilly, sheep-studded countryside, close to the Ochil Hills—hills formed from slag which in Polly's childhood were lit at night by the flames of an iron foundry—and with the blue and purple Pentland Hills in the distance. I saw the stone schoolhouse where she went to school, and the church where she married John Wilson, the love of her life. In that churchyard, many people in this story are buried.

In the village of Kilncadzow (Kilkeggie), I learned that the corner of Portage and Main in Winnipeg is not the windiest place in the world. Apart from a few newer bungalows, it looks as it must have looked when Polly Wilson kissed her children good-bye and departed on the quest that would end in a culvert so many miles away. The land slopes away on all sides of the village, and the vista looking toward the distant Tinto Hill is moody but beautiful.

In my research at the New Register House in Edinburgh, I found that John and Polly Wilson's daughter, Helen (or Ella), was still living at age eighty-three. She had lived all her life close to her grandparents' home, which told me that they had likely raised the Wilson children.

Polly Wilson's parents did indeed raise the two Wilson children, Helen told me, and apart from this terrible tragedy in their lives, they wanted for nothing. "No one can imagine what it's been like to live with this all my life," she said.

Sadly, William Hutchison, broken-hearted about Polly's fate, died December 8, 1921, just two years after hearing that his daughter's husband had murdered her. He was seventy-two. Polly's mother, Helen Hutchison, died March 7, 1935, at the age of eighty-two. James Hutchison was present at both deaths, and he signed the death certificates.

Elizabeth Craig, whose persistence finally opened the case into Polly's disappearance, died December 10, 1965. She was eighty-seven.

"My aunt Elizabeth was a very strong woman," Polly's daughter said. I was not surprised. Archie Craig died in 1949 at the age of seventy-one.

George Wilson, the son who "followed his father everywhere" and whom Jack Wilson left behind at the age of three, died in his early forties of complications from surgery. George Wilson left no descendants.

Polly's daughter, married at age twenty-seven, also had no children. "There are no descendants," Helen said. "It ends with us."

Jessie Patterson married again and bore six more children. She had a full life, active in church, music and community affairs, but she went through periods of deep sadness when she withdrew from the family. She died in her eighties. Her eldest son, born seventy-five years ago today, is still living.

It feels appropriate to finish this book on the anniversary of the day the real story ended.

Lois Simmie
April 23, 1995

∽ INDEX ∾